NUMBER ONE PROBLEM IN
MARRIAGES TODAY . . .
so say many specialists in family relations, is not . . .

sex . . .

money . . .

children . . .

but lack of communication between husband and wife.
H. Norman Wright, associate professor of Psychology at Biola College and Talbot Theological Seminary and a practicing marriage counselor, agrees that lack of communication is the real problem behind skyrocketing divorce rates in the church and out . . .
and he's done something about it by developing practical ideas for communication in marriage that are based squarely on Biblical teaching.

COMMUNICATION: COMMUNICATION: COMMUNICATION: KEY TO YOUR MARRIAGE

H. Norman Wright

GL Regal Books A Division of G/L Publications
Glendale, California, U.S.A.

Other Regal books by H. Norman Wright . . .
Help! I'm a Camp Counselor
The Pillars of Marriage

The foreign language publishing of all Regal books is under the direction of GLINT. GLINT provides financial and technical help for the adaptation, translation and publishing of books in more than 85 languages for millions of people worldwide.

For more information write: GLINT, 110 W. Broadway, Glendale, CA 91204.

Scripture quotations are designated . . .
NASB: New American Standard Bible. © The Lockman Foundation 1960, 1962, 1963, 1968, 1971. Used by permission.
AMP: Amplified Bible, The. Copyright © 1962, 1964 by Zondervan Publishing House. Used by permission.
TLB: From *The Living Bible*. Copyright © 1971 by Tyndale House Publishers, Wheaton, Illinois. Used by permission.
Phillips, THE NEW TESTAMENT IN MODERN ENGLISH, Revised Edition, J.B. Phillips, Translator. © J.B. Phillips 1958, 1960, 1972. Used by permission of Macmillan Publishing Co., Inc.

Eleventh Printing, 1980

Published by
Regal Books Division, G/L Publications
Glendale, California 91209
Printed in U.S.A.

Library of Congress Catalog Card No. 73-88317
ISBN 0-8307-0726-3

contents

A leader's guide for group study with *Communication: Key to Your Marriage* is available from your local church supplier.

foreword

Let us face it. In recent years marriage has been getting "bad press." That once permanent bastion of security and " 'til death do us part" commitment has become for too many an impermanent gamble lasting " 'til divorce seems convenient."

In the church or out, the problems are there. The ardor, enthusiasm and excitement of courtship fade into a grey routine of work, raising kids, and sitting glassy-eyed in front of the tube until the eleven o'clock news signs off. Life grinds on and inevitably there is a decline in understanding as the communication gap grows wider and wider. Many couples lack the elementary communication skills needed to produce the understanding necessary for a marriage to grow strong, or even exist, in these times of "swapping, swinging and shacking."

What can be done? Is there a way to make marriage work better—or work at all? What about the ideal called "Christian marriage"? Is a Christian marriage possible today?

Books on marriage and marriage problems abound. This book is designed to take you beyond the problems and start working on the solutions. Real communication between husband and wife is possible. Over the last several years Norm

Wright has proved it—in classes, seminars, workshops, retreats—wherever he can get a group of married (or planning to be married) people together.

As a practicing marriage counselor, licensed in California, Norm has the experience and background to speak with authority on marital problems and why lack of communication is at the bottom of most of them.

As one of the most popular professors in his seminary and a much-in-demand speaker and teacher across the land, he has the educational know-how to do what this book is all about—communicate.

One of the best things about this book is that it's more than a book. It's an experience in learning, sharing and communicating. You don't simply read this book; you dialogue with it—and, hopefully, with your partner. You don't just talk about communicating. You *do* it—perhaps for the first time.

Don't just "dip into" this book. Jump in with both feet. Interact with the "What Do You Think?" and "What's Your Plan?" sections in each chapter. Above all, interact with your mate and *communicate,* more deeply, personally and honestly than you ever have before. Communication is the key to *your* marriage.

Fritz Ridenour

INTRODUCTION

marriage: the only game both players can win!

Does the institution called "marriage" have a future? Some experts are saying that marriage as we now know it is on the way out. As divorce rates continue to climb, or at least stay at appallingly high levels, many people, in and out of the church, are growing pessimistic about marriage. Even for seemingly "perfectly matched" couples, marriage grows to be more and more of a gamble.

There are three major changes taking place in the institution of marriage today:

1. A decline in understanding between marriage partners.
2. The loss of determination to stay married.
3. The development of unrealistic marriage expectations.

Decline of understanding and lack of communication go together. Many couples today lack the kind of communication skills that produce the understanding necessary for a marriage to grow strong, or even exist. Understanding in a marriage doesn't mean that there are no differences. It does mean that you and your mate are able to talk about the differences and come to an understanding of each other's views. You are able to accept the fact that your partner was raised in a different fashion and because of that will react differently than you. Just because something was done in a certain manner in your home when you were growing up does not mean that it has to be done that same way in your new home.

Two people who love one another but are unable to understand each other suffer pain—a continual biting pain in their relationship. Understanding may not come easily, but a willingness to share views, to see the "other side of the question," to talk things out can help a husband and wife adjust and adapt to their honest differences of opinion.

Someone has likened this adjustment to two porcupines who lived in Alaska. When the deep and heavy snows came they felt the cold and began to draw close together. However, when they drew close they began to stick one another with their quills. When they drew apart they felt the cold once again. In order to keep warm they had to learn how to adjust to one another.

Lack of determination to stay married is seen today on every hand. To have had more than one husband or wife is not considered at all unusual. As one woman filled out an application for a new job, she came to the question, "Married or Single?" Her answer: "Between marriages."

Many enter marriage today with the attitude that if they do not get along they can break the relationship and try again. Many people are too impatient with their marriages. They do not want to live "happily ever after." They want to

"WHEN I GOT MARRIED
I WAS LOOKING FOR AN IDEAL—
THEN IT BECAME AN ORDEAL
AND NOW I WANT A NEW DEAL."

live "happily right away" and when this does not happen, they bail out.

Too many young couples enter marriage blinded by unrealistic expectations. They believe the relationship should be characterized by a high level of continuous romantic love. As one young adult said: "I wanted marriage to fulfill all my desires. I needed security, someone to take care of me, intellectual stimulation, economic security immediately—but it just wasn't like that!" People are looking for something "magical" to happen in marriage.

But magic doesn't make a marriage work: hard work does. When there are positive results it is because of two people working together one step at a time.

One rather cynical description of marriage is that it is "the only game of chance at which both players can lose." I prefer to see it as the only game in which both players can win! I agree wholeheartedly with Richard Lessor, when he writes in his book, *Love, Marriage and Trading Stamps:* "It isn't a case of marriage having been tried and found wanting. In the twentieth century world, true marriage is deeply wanted but largely untried."(1)

And how do you go about trying "true marriage"? It will do little good to look to society for help. Society struggles with the crisis but continues to become hopelessly entangled in its own web of conflicting values and ideas. Society seeks answers but only provides more and more questions.

Is the whole thing hopeless? Not at all. Society has not provided a way to a truly happy marriage, but God has! God has given a definite pattern for marriage and if a man and woman will follow that pattern, they will find the happiness and harmony they seek.

Charles Shedd in his book, *Letters to Phillip,* tells the story of two rivers flowing smoothly and quietly along until they came together and joined. When this happened they clashed and hurled themselves at one another. As the newly formed river flowed downstream, however, it gradually quieted down and flowed smoothly again. But now it was much broader, more majestic and had much more power. Dr. Shedd suggests that "A good marriage is often like that. When two independent streams of existence come together, there will probably be some dashing of life against life at the juncture. Personalities rush against each other. Preferences clash. Ideas contend for power and habits vie for position. Sometimes like the waves, they throw up a spray that leaves you breathless and makes you wonder where has the loveliness gone. But that's all right. Like the two rivers, what comes out of their struggle may be something deeper, more powerful than what they were on their own."(2)

Two Christians have the best possibilities for a happy marriage because they have a third Person—the Lord Jesus Christ—working with them and strengthening them. But there *must* be communication—between them and their Lord and between themselves. That's what the rest of this book is all about. Truly, communication—with Christ and each other—is the key to your marriage.

CHAPTER 1

what is a "Christian" marriage?

As you read this chapter, you will discover . . .

. . . the definition of a Christian marriage

. . . what it means to be "one flesh"

. . . how to evaluate your own marriage and take steps to enrich and improve it.

How would you describe being married? What do you think of when you hear the word "marriage"? Joy, love, happiness, bliss? Misery, hatred, frustration? Or just boredom and the blahs?

Definitions of marriage are a dime a dozen, and a lot of them don't seem to put much more value on marriage than that!

Meander said, "Marriage, if one will face the truth, is an evil, but a necessary evil."

Montaigne said, "Marriage happens as with cages: the birds without despair to get in and those within despair of getting out."

Sidney Smith's statement about marriage is clever, yet contains a great deal of wisdom. He said, "Marriage resembles a pair of shears, so joined that they cannot be separated; often moving in opposite directions, yet always punishing anyone who comes between them."

WHAT DO YOU THINK? #1

The definitions of marriage given above have touches of cynicism or at least satire. What is *your* definition of marriage? Write it below.

Marriage: A Contract with an Escape Clause?

Some psychologists, marriage counselors and ministers have suggested that marriage is a contract and many people are quick to agree. But is this really true? Is marriage really a contract?

In every contract there are certain conditional clauses. A contract between two parties, whether they be companies or individuals, involves the responsibility of both parties to carry out their part of the bargain. These are CONDITIONAL CLAUSES or "IF CLAUSES." If you do this, the other person must do this, and if the other person does this, you must do this. But in the marriage relationship and the marriage ceremony there are no conditional clauses. Nowhere does the marriage ceremony say, "If the husband loves his wife then the wife continues in the contract." Or, "If the wife is submissive to her husband then the husband carries out the contract." Marriage is an unconditional commitment into which two people enter.

In most contracts there are ESCAPE CLAUSES. An escape clause says that if the party of the first part does not carry out his responsibilities, then the party of the second part is absolved. If one person does not live up to his part of the bargain, the second person can get out of the contract. This is an escape clause. In marriage there is no escape clause.

WHAT DO YOU THINK? #2

Rate yourself on a scale of 1 to 5 (1—very uncomfortable; 2—slightly more comfortable; 3—could be; 4—probably so; 5—sounds good) regarding your response to the following concepts. (Circle the appropriate one.)

1. Marriage is a necessary evil.

   1 2 3 4 5

2. It is normal—even desirable—for marriage partners to be moving in opposite directions in life.

1 2 3 4 5

3. Most couples have unwritten conditional clauses in their marriage that both know about but never discuss.

1 2 3 4 5

4. It would be to your advantage to have an escape clause in the marriage contract to protect you because if the marriage goes sour it will probably be the other person's fault.

1 2 3 4 5

5. Marriage is an unconditional commitment of the total person for total life.

1 2 3 4 5

Marriage: Blending, Not Rending

In his book, *The Essence of Marriage*, ordained minister and marriage counselor Julius A. Fritze describes marriage as follows:

"Marriage is an emotional fusion of two personalities into a functional operation, yet both retaining their own identities. The Biblical concept is contained in Genesis 2:24—'One flesh'." Fritze goes on to illustrate the marriage relationship by talking about two lumps of clay. He points out that if you were to hold a lump of dark green clay in your left hand and a lump of light green clay in your right hand, you could clearly see the different shades. However, if you were to take both of these pieces of clay and mold and push them together, you would see just one lump of green clay—at first glance. But if you were to inspect the lump closely you would see the distinct and separate lines of dark green and light green clay. This is like the marriage relationship—two people blended together so they appear as one, yet each retaining his own distinct identity or personality.(1) It's one new life existing in two people.

Christian marriage, however, involves more than the blending of two people. It also includes a *third Person*—Jesus Christ—who gives meaning, guidance and direction to the relationship. When Jesus Christ presides in a marriage, then and only then is it a Christian marriage.

Various writers have given definitions of "Christian marriage."

Wayne Oates, professor at Southern Baptist Theological Seminary, says: "Marriage is a covenant of responsible love, a fellowship of repentance and forgiveness."

David Augsburger, Mennonite minister and author of *Cherishable: Love and Marriage,* defines marriage by first asking, "Is marriage a private action of two persons in love, or a public act of two pledging a contract?" Then he goes on to say, "Neither. It is something other. Very much other!

"Basically the Christian view of marriage is not that it is primarily or even essentially a binding legal and social contract. The Christian understands marriage as a covenant made under God and in the presence of fellow members of the Christian family. Such a pledge endures, not because of the force of law or the fear of its sanctions, but because an unconditional covenant has been made. A covenant more solemn, more binding, more permanent than any legal contract."(2)

Dwight Small, experienced counselor and author of several books on marriage, defines marriage as: "One new life existent in two persons."

Elton Trueblood, author of *Company of the Committed* and other books on Christian discipleship, calls marriage, "A system by means of which persons who are sinful and contentious are so caught up by a dream and a purpose bigger than themselves that they work through the years, in spite of repeated disappointment, to make the dream come true."

Dr. David Hubbard, president of Fuller Theological Seminary, has said: "Marriage does not demand perfection. But it must be given priority. It is an institution for sinners. No one else need apply. But it finds its fullest glory when sinners see it as God's way of leading us through His ultimate curriculum of love and righteousness."

WHAT DO YOU THINK? #3

From the five definitions of Christian marriage given above, circle the name of the writer whose definition you like the best.

Oates Augsburger Small Trueblood Hubbard

In the definition that you picked as "best" what ideas appeal to you the most?

Of the five definitions of marriage given above, which one appealed to you the least?

Oates Augsburger Small Trueblood Hubbard

What bothers you the most about that definition?

Use the five definitions of Christian marriage, plus your own ideas to compile your own definition of "Christian marriage."

What Does the Bible Say About Marriage?

What, then, are God's purposes for marriage?

One basic purpose is procreation—to bring children into the world. God created man in His own image and then said: "Be fruitful and multiply, and fill the earth, and subdue it . . ." (Gen. 1:28). Psalm 127:3-5 teaches that *"children are a gift of the Lord. . . . like arrows in the hand of a warrior. . . . How blessed is the man whose quiver is full of them" (NASB).*

Procreation also involves providing adequate care and training for your children. *"Train up a child in the way he should go,"* says the well-known verse from Proverbs, *"even when he is old he will not depart from it"* (Prov. 22:6, *NASB*).

But there is much more to marriage than the procreation, care and training of children. Genesis 2:18-25 teaches that marriage was God's idea and that He had several divine purposes in mind.

18. *Then the Lord God said, "It is not good that the man should be alone; I will make him a helper fit for him."*

19. *(So) out of the ground the Lord God formed every beast of the field and every bird of the air, and brought them to the man to see what he would call them; and what-*

ever the man called (every) living creation, that was its name.

20. *The man gave names to all the cattle, and to the birds of the air, and to every beast of the field, but for the man there was not found a helper fit for him.*

21. *So the Lord God caused a deep sleep to fall upon the man, and while he slept took one of his ribs and closed up its place with flesh;*

22. *and the rib which the Lord God had taken from the man he made into a woman and brought her to the man.*

23. *Then the man said, "This at last is bone of my bones and flesh of my flesh; she shall be called Woman, because she was taken out of Man."*

24. *Therefore a man leaves his father and his mother and cleaves to his wife, and they become one flesh.*

25. *And the man and his wife were both naked, and were not ashamed. (RSV)*

God created marriage for *companionship.* As John Milton observed, ". . . Loneliness was the first thing God's eye named not good." Loneliness and isolation are contradictions to the purpose in God's creative act. God made man to live with others, and the first "other" was woman.

God also created marriage for *completeness.* The woman was to be . . . *a helper fit for him* (Gen. 2:18). The woman was created to be a complement or counterpart, suitable for the man. The woman assists man in making his life (and hers, too) complete. She fills up the empty places. She shares his life with him, draws him out of himself and into a wider area of contact through the involvement they have with one another. She is one who can enter into responsible companionship. The partners in a marriage relationship are actually fulfilling God's purpose of completeness or wholeness to life.

The companionship and completeness that God intended for marriage grow out of *communication* as two people share each day and the meaning of their lives. As Dwight

Small says, "The heart of marriage is its communication system. . . . But no couple begins marriage with highly developed communication. It is not something they bring into marriage ready made but something to be continually cultivated through all of the experiences of their shared life."(3) Satisfying companionship and a sense of completeness develop as husband and wife learn to communicate with openness and understanding.

Marriage—a New Relationship

Genesis 2:24 puts an emphasis upon two verbs: *leave* and *cleave*. The word *leave* means to abandon, forsake, to sever one relationship before establishing another. Unfortunately, many individuals do not make this break. They leave home *physically* but remain there *psychologically*. The attachment to home and parents should be replaced by the attachment to one's mate. This does not mean disregarding or dishonoring one's parents, but rather breaking a tie to one's parents and assuming one's own responsibility for a spouse.

The second word, *cleave*, means to weld, grip or adhere together. When a man "cleaves" to his wife, they become *one flesh*. The term "one flesh" is a beautiful capsule description of the oneness, completeness and permanence God intended in the marriage relationship. "One flesh" suggests a unique oneness—a total commitment to intimacy in all of life together, symbolized by sexual union.

The Jewish rabbis taught that man is restless while he misses the rib that was taken out of his side and the woman is restless until she gets under the arm of the man—from where she came. With all of the flap in recent years over women's lib, here is a majestic statement of just how the Bible views woman. She is not man's *property*. She is man's *partner*—a full partner in every sense of the word.

St. Augustine lived in the fifth century, but what he said fits perfectly into today's heated discussions of women's rights. He wrote: "If God meant woman to rule over man,

He would have taken her out of Adam's head. Had He designed her to be his slave, He would have taken her out of his feet. But God took woman out of man's side, for He made her to be a helpmate and an equal to him."

In his book, *After You've Said I Do,* Dwight Small emphasizes the Bible's consistent equalitarian and democratic view of marriage. "There can be no true oneness," writes Small, "except as there is equal dignity and status for both partners. The wife who came from man's side is to stand at his side, to share every responsibility and enjoy every privilege. This is the goal."

Small goes on to admit that achieving this goal is not easy. What is needed is *dialogue.* He believes that "dialogue takes place when two people communicate the full meaning of their lives to one another, when they participate in each other's lives in the most meaningful ways in which they are capable."(4)

From Genesis 2:18-24, you can gather three distinctly Christian views of marriage:

1. As mentioned, marriage is to be permanent, for life. When two become one flesh, there is to be no division, no severing, because of the irreparable damage that will occur.

2. Marriage is to be monogamous. There are examples of polygamy in Scripture, but these are descriptions of what men did, not of what Scripture teaches as good and right. Again, one flesh means one flesh. A man cannot become one flesh with more than one woman and have it mean what is meant here.

3. Finally, Christian marriage demands fidelity. Today's new morality claims that a man can become "one flesh" with as many women as he wishes, that fornication and a little adultery are "healthy" pastimes that broaden experience and deepen relationships.

God's description of marriage, however, speaks of deep and lasting intimacy, a companionship between husband and wife that leads to mutual enrichment, happiness and welfare. Adultery is to marriage what a knife is to a back. Today's advocates of "new morality" can think of all kinds of excuses for adultery and fornication. They come up with what might be called a "pretzel" morality, in which facts, sound principles for good human relationships and responsibilities are all twisted and bent into shapes that seemingly, in some cases, justify infidelity as a "good and loving thing in the situation."

As Dwight Small says in his book, *Design for Christian Marriage,* "A Christian marriage can never fail, but the people in that marriage can fail. There is a vast difference between the two possibilities. So if the marriage of two Christians seems to fail, it is either that they were ignorant of God's purposes, or unwilling to commit themselves to it."(5)

Way back in the beginning God spelled it out. As early as

the second chapter of Genesis, He made it clear that marriage is a *total* commitment of the *total* person for *total* life.

Anything less is not Christian marriage. Anything less can easily fail. But when man and wife come together, committed to God and committed to communicating the full meaning of their lives to each other, they cannot help but succeed.

WHAT'S YOUR PLAN?

If you are studying this book with your spouse, best results can be obtained if you complete the following material individually and then discuss your answers together. As you compare ideas, feelings and attitudes you will achieve new levels of communication and understanding in your marriage.

PART 1

Think back to before you were married . . .

1. What did you think marriage would be like? Did it turn out the way you expected?

2. Did you and your spouse have different expectations for marriage? How did you discover the differences? Have you talked directly about these differences?

3. I expected marriage to change my life-style by . . .

4. I believe my mate expected me to be . . .

5. I expected my mate to be more . . .

PART 2

1. If you were going to describe your marriage at this time with one word, what word would you use?

2. What word do you think your spouse would use to describe your marriage?

3. What benefits are you getting from your marriage relationship that you wouldn't have received if you had remained single? Be very specific.

4. What strengths do you see in your spouse? Have you ever told him or her that you are aware of these strengths and appreciate them?

5. What does your spouse do that makes you feel loved or of value?

6. What do you do that expresses your love and appreciation toward your spouse?

7. What are the strengths in your marriage? Who contributes most of these strengths, you or your spouse?

8. What do you feel is the weakest area in your marriage? In what ways might you be responsible for this weak area?

9. What efforts are you now making to make your marriage a happy one?

10. What efforts do you see your spouse making?

11. What are your present goals for your marriage? What are you going to do to reach these goals? What can you do differently that will enable you to reach them?

Here are some suggestions for you to consider:

- I will show more of an interest in my spouse's activities by asking questions.
- I will spend more time thinking about positive factors in my marriage relationship and attempt to discover ways to be what my spouse wants and needs.
- I will take time to pray for and with my family, especially my spouse.
- If I have any resentments against the family members—and particularly my spouse—I will forgive them now.

Other goals I want to set:

CHAPTER 2

who's in charge here?

As you read this chapter, you will discover . . .
. . . why there is a "leadership vacuum" in many homes today
. . . the Biblical definition of the role of the wife
. . . what it means to submit to your husband
. . . the Biblical definition of the role of the husband
. . . what it means to "love your wife".

In today's world there is some confusion in the role and responsibility of the wife-mother and that of the husband-father. Who is the head of the home or *is* there to be a head?

Imagine a Martian coming to our world and landing in our front yard. He steps out of his spaceship and rings the doorbell at your home. Suppose one of your children opens the door and the Martian says, "Take me to your leader." To whom would the child go? To the father? To the mother? To both? Or would the child say, "I am the leader." Who is the head or leader in your home today?

Jokes and stories abound about the ineffectiveness of the man as a leader. We have heard the statement that behind every successful man stands an understanding and helpful wife. One writer said, "Baloney! Behind every successful man stands a surprised mother-in-law!" Statements and jokes like these are clever and yet for some family situations they are painfully true.

"He brags that he's the boss in his home, but he lies about other things too."

"When she wants his opinion, she gives it to him."

"The only time he opens his mouth is to ask for the apron, and the vacuum cleaner."

She snaps, "Are you a man or a mouse?—squeak up!"

"The last big decision she let him make was whether to wash or dry."

Today there seems to be a new husband-father image. Basically the man has assumed the role of financial provider in the family (this, too, is changing in many homes!) and leaves all of the other functions to his wife. Many men appear to be assistants to their wives in areas that once were their responsibility. In most marriages the couple begins by sharing interest and responsibilities; then specialization gradually gets in. The man becomes engrossed with his job (the economic side of life) and neglects his other responsibilities. The wife is left in charge or simply "takes charge" because of the leadership vacuum.

Another factor contributing heavily to the "leadership gap" is a belief by many families in what they think is "pure democracy". Everyone in the family, including the children, casts an equal vote. Is this proper? Is this what the Scripture teaches? Many so-called "Christian" homes today are on the verge of disintegration because of the lack of a leader. They are on shaky ground because they purposely choose to ignore the guidelines that have been set down for them in Scripture.

WHAT DO YOU THINK? #4

1. According to the preceding paragraphs, there is a lack of male leadership in many homes because the husband becomes engrossed in his career and making money and neglects his other responsibilities. From what you have experienced and observed, would you agree?

2. List some responsibilities you think husbands tend to neglect because of their involvement in their career.

What Is the Biblical Role of the Wife?

Ephesians 5:22-33 contains the clearest Biblical definition of marriage roles. In Ephesians 5:22-24 Paul speaks particularly to the wife about her responsibilities to her husband:

You wives must submit to your husband's leadership in

the same way you submit to the Lord. For a husband is in charge of his wife in the same way Christ is in charge of his body the church. (He gave his very life to take care of it and be its Savior!) So you wives must willingly obey your husbands in everything, just as the church obeys Christ (TLB).

Genesis 2:18-20 teaches that the woman was created to be a "helpmeet," one who is to be a complement to the man and assist him. In a real sense the wife is a fulfillment of the husband's life.

Ephesians 5:22-24 teaches that the wife is to be "subject" or "submissive" to her husband. How are these two concepts wed together? How can the wife be a "completer" of her husband and also be submissive to him? What does this mean in a practical sense?

First, a wife's submission to her husband is from complete freedom and love, not from compulsion or fear. The Church submits to the Lordship of Christ on a voluntary basis—in response to His love. The wife's motivation in submitting to her husband should be the same.

But what does it mean to submit? It does not mean to "be a doormat." The Scriptures say submit, but they do not say "sell out." The wife is *not* to become a nothing, a pawn in her husband's hand. She retains her distinctiveness as an individual with the right to her own ideas and feelings. She is not a servant. She remains a person with a distinct personality and personal needs. She needs to accept responsibility and make decisions as much as her husband does.

The marriage relationship functions smoothly when the Biblical guidelines are followed. Traffic laws enable a driver to reach his destination with the least possible chance of accident or injury. Biblical guidelines help a couple reach their destination of a happy, growing relationship. One of these guidelines is for the wife to submit to her husband as the leader in their relationship. She submits to her husband not because he demands it but because Christ directs her to

in His Word. Lack of submission to her husband is as much a spiritual problem as it is a marital problem!

The wife encourages and strengthens her husband's masculine leadership role and *never* tries to destroy, usurp, weaken or eliminate it. A wife is to respect her husband and affirm his leadership.

Dwight Small suggests that "each is an active participant in building the relationship. . . . Precluded forever is any assumption of superiority-inferiority." He (Paul) affirms the principle of "personal interdependency in marriage."(1)

"God has charged the husband with headship," writes Gladys Hunt. "In fact, he hangs the responsibility of the Fall on the man *(as by one man sin entered the world; the woman was deceived but not the man).* He now makes the husband the head of his wife. He says to the wife, 'Don't make it rough for him. Help him to be what I want him to be. Support him in his role; don't compete for headship.'

"That does not mean that she never has an original thought, never says she disagrees, etc. It does mean that her spirit is controlled by God's Spirit. She doesn't have to prove her worth by grabbing her husband's job."(2)

WHAT DO YOU THINK? #5

Do you agree or disagree that . . .

1. It was God's idea that a wife should immediately give up everything to go with her husband.
   a. Agree strongly
   b. Agree with reservations
   c. Disagree strongly
   d. Disagree with reservations

2. It is all right for an obedient wife to instruct and give advice to her husband.
   a. Agree strongly
   b. Agree with reservations
   c. Disagree strongly
   d. Disagree with reservations

3. A wife has the right to disobey her husband when she feels he is dictating to her.
   a. Agree strongly
   b. Agree with reservations
   c. Disagree strongly
   d. Disagree with reservations

4. Since the wife is assigned the subordinate position in marriage, she is not on an equal basis with man.
   a. Agree strongly
   b. Agree with reservations
   c. Disagree strongly
   d. Disagree with reservations

5. The wife is to be regarded as the one who does the cooking, washing, training of the children, and at the same time she is to be a "helpmeet" to her husband.

a. Agree strongly
b. Agree with reservations
c. Disagree strongly
d. Disagree with reservations

Now, rewrite on another sheet each of the statements to indicate your own belief and convictions.

And What About the Husband's Role?

In Ephesians 5:25-32 Paul deals specifically with the husband's responsibilities:

And you husbands, show the same kind of love to your wives as Christ showed to the church when he died for her, to make her holy and clean, washed by baptism and God's Word; so that he could give her to himself as a glorious church without a single spot or wrinkle or any other blemish, being holy and without a single fault. That is how husbands should treat their wives, loving them as parts of themselves. For since a man and his wife are now one, a man is really doing himself a favor and loving himself when he loves his wife! No one hates his own body but lovingly cares for it, just as Christ cares for his body the church, of which we are parts.

(That the husband and wife are one body is proved by the Scripture which says, "A man must leave his father and mother when he marries, so that he can be perfectly joined to his wife, and the two shall be one.") I know this is hard to understand, but it is an illustration of the way we are parts of the body of Christ (TLB).

In Ephesians 5:23 Paul declares that the husband is the

head of the wife. Unfortunately, too many men only read that much of the Scripture and fail to read the rest of the verse—"as Christ is the Head of the church." Authority is given to the man, but Paul did not mean that husbands should be bosses over their wives. Being the head does not mean being the victor in a struggle. The husband sets the pace by being a leader. The authority is there but he is always answerable to God for his use of it.

As the husband submits to Christ, his authority is transformed by Christ into sacrificial care. The basic truth of this passage is *not* control and domination, but sacrificial love for the wife. The husband is nowhere given the prerogative to rule with a rod of iron. He may *not* impose his own selfish will upon his wife and overshadow her feelings. He is not to demand leadership. The Scripture does not emphasize that Jesus Christ dominates or dictates to the Church. Christ gave Himself for the Church. He takes the initiative to love and serve the Church; *this is the pattern that husbands are to follow in caring for their wives.* When a husband does not do this, he has a spiritual problem (disobedience to the Word) as well as a marital problem.

A loving husband is willing to give all that is required to fulfill the life of his wife. His love is ready to make any sacrifice for her good. The man's first responsibility is to his wife. His love for her enables him to give himself to her.

His love is also a purifying love. The husband never asks his wife to do something which would degrade or harm her. His caring love for his wife is compared to his love for his own body. A man certainly cares for and nourishes his own body. A loving husband does not try to extract service from his wife nor does he make sure that his own physical comfort is assured; he does not love her for the sake of convenience. He does not regard his wife as a kind of permanent servant who simply cooks, washes and trains the children. Rather, the loving husband sees his wife as a person whom he is to cherish and strengthen. A caring love is a serving

NOT "I WILL IF YOU WILL" BUT "WE WILL REGARDLESS"

love. A husband's love is to be patterned after the caring love of Christ.

WHAT DO YOU THINK? #6

Do you agree or disagree that . . .

1. The Scripture teaches that the husband is the head of the family. Thus, the wife should be submissive and obedient to her husband in everything even if he is an unbeliever.

   a. Agree strongly
   b. Agree with reservations
   c. Disagree strongly
   d. Disagree with reservations

2. Since man is the head of the family, and this headship is patterned after that of Christ, therefore, the husband should be the "boss" of his wife.

   a. Agree strongly
   b. Agree with reservations
   c. Disagree strongly
   d. Disagree with reservations

3. It is all right for the husband to demand obedience or order his wife to respect his authority.

   a. Agree strongly
   b. Agree with reservations
   c. Disagree strongly
   d. Disagree with reservations

4. Usually the husband should make the final decision when he and his wife cannot agree upon a decision that must be made.

   a. Agree strongly
   b. Agree with reservations
   c. Disagree strongly
   d. Disagree with reservations

Now, rewrite on a separate sheet each of the statements to indicate your own belief and conviction.

Where Do We Go from Here?

As you study Ephesians 5:22-33 you should remember to apply these truths in a *very personal and specific way.* Do not concern yourself with your partner's role. Concentrate on your *own responsibility* in your marriage, according to what God's Word teaches. We all like to apply the Scriptures to "someone else." Applying it personally often gets too close to home. And in Ephesians 5 Paul is "close to home," indeed.

For example, some wives react to Paul's teaching in Ephesians by saying, "I will submit to my husband if he does his part and loves me the way I want to be loved."

But in Ephesians 5:21-24 Paul doesn't say that. Paul says to wives, in so many words. "Forget what the man is to do and concern yourself with your own responsibility. Don't base your attitudes and actions on the idea that if your husband does one thing you will do another. Your attitudes and actions are to be the result of your commitment and obedience to Christ, who should be at the center of your marriage."

The same thing is true for husbands. Some men take Paul's teaching and deduce that, "I'm boss in my house. My wife has to obey me. Scripture is on my side."

But notice in Ephesians 5:22-33 Paul does not emphasize the husband's *authority* over his wife. Instead Paul focuses on the husband's *responsibility* to have a self-giving love for his wife. A master illustrator, Paul reminds the husband that he loves his own body; does he love his wife as much? Christ loved His "body," the Church. He set the example that the husband is to follow.

As the husband, you do not demand obedience. You do not order your wife to respect your authority. You do not say, "You be submissive and obedient and *then* I will love you as Scripture tells me to." Instead, you focus on your responsibility to give love. You *give your wife the freedom to decide to submit to you.* Submission, according to Paul, is her responsibility, not yours. And, of course, as she submits, she returns your love freely and joyfully, *because she knows she is loved.*

In Ephesians 5:33 Paul puts his teaching into one capsule statement:

So again I say, a man must love his wife as a part of him self; and the wife must see to it that she deeply respects her husband—obeying, praising and honoring him (TLB). Husband or wife, here is the blueprint for a truly happy marriage. Meet your responsibility and give your mate the freedom to meet his or hers. Then you will build a marriage in which both partners are free to communicate openly and honestly. With good communication, there will be no leadership gap. As husband and wife fulfill their respective Biblical roles, love and submission intertwine. The result is an atmosphere of trust and security where both partners grow and mature as God intends.

WHAT'S YOUR PLAN?

If you are studying this book with your spouse, best results can be obtained if you complete the following material individually and then discuss your answers together. As you compare ideas, feelings and attitudes you will achieve new levels of communication and understanding in your marriage.

Set aside time this week to study Ephesians 5:22-33. Read the passage two or three times and then complete the following:

1. List the instructions given to the wife. Describe in detail what these instructions mean as far as you are concerned.

2. List the instructions given to the husband. Describe in detail what the instructions mean to you.

3. What do you feel will be the consequences if one or the other marriage partner fails to follow these instructions? Be specific.

4. How do you feel the guidelines given in Ephesians 5:22-33 match with the attitudes of marriage partners in today's world?

5. What changes or additions to your life-style do you feel you should make to measure up to the instructions given in Ephesians 5:22-33? Describe these changes and additions in some detail.

A husband might say:

I can show more love by asking my wife where she would like to go on our next vacation.

I can consider her feelings and opinions when it comes time to decide on that new car.

I can sit down and talk to my wife about something that interests her.

I can tell her that I love her.

Add your own ideas of things you want to say and changes you want to make. . . .

A wife might say:

I can seek to discover the needs of my husband and see that they are met.

I can watch my tone of voice when he comes home late from work and hasn't called to tell me he will be late.

I can support him more by encouraging and building him up in areas where confidence is lacking.

Add your own ideas of things you want to say and changes you want to make. . . .

CHAPTER 3

how do you make it work?

As you read this chapter, you will discover . . .

. . . the "when," "how," and "who" of decision making in a marriage

. . . principles from 1 Peter 3 concerning the role of the husband and the role of the wife

. . . how to make changes in your attitudes or behavior that will build a stronger marriage.

Ephesians 5 makes it clear. The husband is to be the loving leader of the home. His wife is to lovingly submit to his leadership. These are great prinicples, but how do they work out in the nitty-gritty situations of daily life? For example, what about the dozens of decisions that must be made each day?

According to family specialist Nathan Ackerman, "Delineation of the expected family role functions of male and female is often unclear. Issues of cooperation, division of labor, and sharing of authority are consequently confused. Each parent competes with the other and fears being bested. Neither is sure, yet each pretends to superior competence. Paradoxically each passes the buck to the other for the responsibility of decisions. The strife of competition reduces empathic sympathy, distorts communications, impairs the mutuality of support and sharing and decreases satisfaction of personal need. In effect, intelligent cooperation lessens, and bickering and recrimination mount. The inevitable consequence is progressive emotional alienation in parental relations.

"With the father absent much of the day, the mother assumes the dominant position in the home.

"The father strives mightily to show success as a man. He pursues what has been called 'the suicidal cult of manliness.' To prove his merit, it is not enough to be a man; he must be a superman. In his daily work, he serves some giant industrial organization, or he is a lone wolf in the jungle warfare of modern competitive enterprise. The more he succeeds, the more he dreads failure. He brings his work worries home. Depleted by his exertions, he has little emotional stamina left over to give freely of his love to wife and children.

"He wants to be buttressed for the war of tomorrow, but he finds his wife absorbed in her own busy life. He feels deserted and alone and angry that his wife gives him so little understanding. She reproaches him for not taking a more responsible role in the family. She demands more consideration for herself and the children. For the difficulties with the children she feels guilty. But she denies this guilt and projects it to father. Father takes it. He thinks it must really be his fault. Though confused and angry, he appeases mother because of his need for her. He tries to be useful to win her favor.

"Both parents therefore act unnatural. They are suspicious of any open show of emotion, which they regard as weakness. A free flow of emotion is felt to be dangerous, as if all emotion were equated with something bad and destructive. Therefore it must be curbed. Anxiety over loss of control is constant. Tender sentiment is avoided or, if expressed, is ignored; it spells weakness and the threat of loss of control. Thus the behavior of both parents becomes overcontrolled, unspontaneous, and reduced in vitality. Both parents are burdened with anxiety, guilt and doubt. They are afraid of life and have lost their zest for play and sense of adventure. They settle down to a stereotyped way of living, a safe conforming routine. They strive to live up to the Joneses with all the external accoutrements of conventional success—a home, a new car, the latest gadgets."(1)

WHAT DO YOU THINK? #7

1. How do you feel about who makes the decisions in your family? (Circle the appropriate statements.)
   a. I feel comfortable about who makes the decisions.
   b. I don't like to make decisions.
   c. I feel I make too many decisions.
   d. I feel that I don't make enough decisions.
   e. I am reluctant to give up making any of the decisions I now make.
   f. Decisions? What decisions?

Who Is Responsible?

Unclear roles and confusion over who is responsible for things like making decisions, disciplining the children, or handling the money, do cause many marriage problems. But how can a husband and wife know what to do about decision making and other practical "who is responsible?" problems?

James Jauncey, in his book *Magic in Marriage,* points out that the Christian husband and wife have specific help for everyday problems, not only from the guidelines in Scripture, but also in the daily presence of the Holy Spirit. As Jauncey says, "God through His Holy Spirit seeks our best welfare and happiness. He seldom does this by a supernatural act. Instead, He seeks to permeate our thinking until our judgments are His.

"In marriage He has two people to work through. The husband's authority does not carry infallibility with it. Since the two have become 'one flesh' the guidance has to come through both. This means that except in cases of emergency, decisions affecting the whole family should not be put into effect until they are unanimous."(2)

This view is also held by Lionel Whiston. In his book *Are You Fun to Live With?* he says, "By far the most productive and ideal method of dealing with decisions is to make them together under God. This rules out the possibility of taking over areas of responsibility in open defiance, in secret, by emotional blackmail, or by constantly placating the offended partner.

"The prelude to making joint decisions under God is the commitment of the partners to Him, as individuals and as a team. It relies on wisdom and direction greater than that of either partner, claimed by faith. Practically, it means examining all the factors involved, 'putting the cards on the table,' including pertinent data, inner motives and desires, the recognition of which spouse has greater experience in the particular area, and lessons learned in the past."(3)

This view presupposes that both individuals are honestly and truthfully seeking the will of God for their lives and are completely willing to follow the will of God. Many times a husband and wife decide that it is better for one or the other to make decisions in different areas of responsibility. Many a wise husband, realizing the capabilities and strengths of his wife, has delegated definite responsibilities and authority where the wife can best complement him. Each relies upon the strength and wisdom of the other person. What happens when the husband and wife cannot agree upon a decision that must be made? In cases like this perhaps the husband should decide. This does not mean it will be the best decision but God will hold the man responsible for the decision, not the woman.

For Biblical guidelines in working out decisions together, a passage with many specific practical suggestions is 1 Peter 3:1-9, where the apostle Peter talks about what marriage partners should do and be. Peter completes chapter 2 of his first letter with a stirring description of how Christ submitted Himself to sacrifice and suffering. He set a personal example that all Christians should follow. (See 1 Pet. 2:21.) Then Peter opens chapter 3 with practical applications of how to follow Christ's example by saying:

1. *In the same way, you wives, be submissive to your own husbands so that even if any of them are disobedient to the word, they may be won without a word by the behavior of their wives,*

2. *as they observe your chaste and respectful behavior.*

3. *And let not your adornment be external only—braiding the hair, and wearing gold jewelry, and putting on dresses;*

4. *but let it be the hidden person of the heart, with the imperishable quality of a gentle and quiet spirit, which is precious in the sight of God.*

5. *For in this way in former times the holy women also,*

who hoped in God, used to adorn themselves, being submissive to their own husbands.

6. *Thus Sarah obeyed Abraham, calling him lord, and you have become her children if you do what is right without being frightened by any fear.*

7. *You husbands likewise, live with your wives in an understanding way, as with a weaker vessel, since she is a woman; and grant her honor as a fellow-heir of the grace of life, so that your prayers may not be hindered.*

8. *To sum up, let all be harmonious, sympathetic, brotherly, kind-hearted, and humble in spirit;*

9. *not returning evil for evil, or insult for insult, but giving a blessing instead; for you were called for the very purpose that you might inherit a blessing (NASB).*

Why So Much Advice for Wives?

It is interesting that the advice Peter gives to the wives in this passage is six times as long as his advice to the husbands. There is a reason for this. At the time Peter wrote, if the husband became a Christian his wife automatically followed him into the church. But if the wife became a believer, it created tensions and difficulties. In Peter's day, men and women did not hold equal places in the family.

This inequality was even reflected in the Jewish form of morning prayer. One of the sentences that a Jewish man prayed each morning was, "I thank God that He did not make me a Gentile, or slave or a woman." The view of women that permeated all of the Jewish law was that the woman was not a person, but a thing. She had no legal rights; she was absolutely in her husband's possession to do with her as he pleased!

Now, in theory the Jews had a high ideal of marriage. The rabbis said, "Every Jew must surrender his life rather than commit idolatry, murder or adultery." "The very altar sheds tears when a man divorces the wife of his youth."

That was theory! The fact was, that in the time of Christ, divorce was tragically easy!

The divorce laws at that time were strange. The wife had no rights of divorce at all, unless her husband became a leper, an apostate or engaged in a "disgusting trade." But under the law a man could divorce his wife for almost any cause. The woman was helpless and defenseless. And the entire process of obtaining a divorce was very easy. The law said that a man who wished a divorce had to hand his wife a bill of divorcement which read, "Let this be from me your letter of divorce and letter of dismissal and deed of liberation, that you may marry whatever man you want." The husband handed the bill of divorcement to his wife in the presence of two witnesses and the marriage was over.

In the Greek world at the time of Christ the situation was worse. Women of the respectable classes in Greece led a completely secluded life. They took no part in public life; they never appeared on the streets alone; they never even appeared at meals or at social occasions. Each woman had her own living quarters and no one but her husband might enter. It was the man's job to keep the woman secluded so she might see as little as possible, hear as little as possible and ask as little as possible. Companionship and fellowship in marriage were unheard of in that day. A man found these pleasures outside of marriage.

Peter has all these conditions in mind as he talks to the ladies about how to be good wives, even if they are Christians and their husbands are not. His advice isn't profound; it is surprisingly simple. Be a good wife. That is all. Nothing more. Nothing less. By the silent preaching of her behavior the Christian wife will win her husband.

Many Christian women have fallen into the trap of being a walking tape recorder. They virtually remember every word of the pastor's sermon and when they get home they parrot what they have heard. Other women, in their efforts to reach their husbands for Christ, mention God in every statement and the husband feels that a normal conversation is a rarity. He even gets a sermon out of how God created the wonderful cows which makes it possible for him to have steak on his plate!

A wife accomplishes more by her Christian behavior than by what she says. As one woman stated, "I haven't told my husband that I've accepted the Lord. I want to wait until he sees such a change in me that he will ask, 'What's going on with you? Why are you so different?' Then when I tell him it will make sense."

Peter goes on to explain how a wife is to be a good wife. She is to be submissive. This means she is voluntarily unselfish. A good wife is also pure and respectful. A respectful wife is one who tries never to say or do anything that embarrasses her husband or makes him feel unsure or ashamed. She is concerned about his welfare, building him up instead of tearing him down. A good wife is worthy of being trusted. She is faithful and doesn't engage in what some call "innocent flirtations."

A third principle from this passage is that a quality wife knows what to wear. As Peter wrote this he was not telling women how to dress. He was simply giving a principle: a beautiful woman is one who has an inner beauty and radiance.

As William Coleman says, "Naturally, within reason a woman wants to look both contemporary and attractive. But she does not want to appear brash. To many young women the emphasis seems to be sexuality. What a shame if they never understand femininity!

"Do you know how a female rhino selects her male rhino? She is nearsighted, so when she sees her beau she first backs up. Then she charges him at thirty miles an hour, hitting him broadside and knocking him to the ground. Then she proceeds to gouge and step on him. While he is literally bleeding and bruised he gets the message, 'she loves me!'

"The Christian woman is not this way. She is feminine.

She is gentle, sweet and kind because she knows what femininity is all about. There are very few men who would want a drill sergeant for a wife."(4)

Peter didn't want the Christian woman to demand attention just because she was a woman. Instead he encouraged her to develop an inner beauty that reflects femininity, gentleness, thoughtfulness and love.

WHAT DO YOU THINK? #8

(For Wives Only)

1. First Peter 3:1-6 gives several specific suggestions how a wife can live out her role in the marriage relationship. To apply this passage to yourself, complete the following sentences:

I am submissive to my husband when I . . .

I respect my husband when I . . .

I show a gentle and quiet spirit when I . . .

2. Following are four of Peter's words to wives. Which ones say something to you about decision making in your marriage? Why?

Submissive

Respectful

Gentle

Quiet

3. Do Peter's words to wives—submissive, respectful, gentle and quiet—indicate that you are to always let your husband make the decisions in your family? Why? Why not?

4. Circle the feelings that are a part of you:

I listen to my husband comfortably.

Always Sometimes Seldom Never

I wish my husband would listen more to my ideas.

Always Sometimes Seldom Never

I really have the best understanding of how to handle discipline with the children.

Always Sometimes Seldom Never

I think it's important to let my husband feel he's the leader even if I do most of the planning.

Always Sometimes Seldom Never

Wives today should not be expected to actually obey their husbands.

Always Sometimes Seldom Never

I enjoy knowing that my husband is the leader in our family; it makes me feel safe.

Always Sometimes Seldom Never

I wish my husband would help me more with handling the money.

Always Sometimes Seldom Never

Peter Talks to Husbands

The apostle Peter takes only one brief paragraph—1 Peter 3:7—to speak to the husbands, but in that paragraph

WIVES APPRECIATE CONSIDERATION AND UNDERSTANDING

he gives much valuable advice. In fact, Peter gives the husbands three principles to live by.

First, a husband must be understanding. This means he is willing to listen to his wife's point of view. He's willing to think with her. He is sensitive to her feelings, moods and ideas. He tries to discover his wife's needs in order to meet them and do what is best for her. Here we see the selfless attitude being important in the husband's role as well as in the role of the wife.

Second, the husband is to be a protector. Recognizing that his wife is not as rugged physically as he is, the Christian husband is not to let his wife overwork. He knows when to take her out for dinner, or even away for the weekend without the kids. (This is good for both husband and wife!) Also, the husband doesn't let the children get away with being disrespectful to their mother. He treats his wife with respect, love and consideration, and protects her from hurtful situations.

In the third place, Peter tells husbands to remember that wives have spiritual rights that are equal to theirs. They are joint-heirs of God's grace. God loves wives just as much as He loves husbands.

What happens if husbands do not follow the instructions in 1 Peter 3? Peter explains one significant consequence. He says, "Otherwise, you won't be able to pray." In other words, if your relationship isn't right with others it won't be right with God.

WHAT DO YOU THINK? #9

(For Husbands Only)

1. First Peter 3:7 gives specific suggestions for how a husband can live out his role in the marriage relationship. To apply this passage to yourself, complete the following:

I show consideration and understanding for my wife by . . .

I honor her and protect her by . . .

I treat my wife as my spiritual equal by . . .

2. Following are the three key statements Peter makes to husbands. What do they say to you about decision making in your marriage?

Be understanding

Be a protector

Know that God loves your wife as much as He loves you.

3. If you are an understanding protector who knows God loves your wife as much as He loves you, does this suggest you are to make all the decisions in your family? Why? Why not?

4. Check the feelings that are a part of you:

I listen to my wife comfortably.

Always Sometimes Seldom Never

My wife has outlandish ideas.

Always Sometimes Seldom Never

I wish my wife would listen more to me and my ideas.

Always Sometimes Seldom Never

I am afraid that my role of disciplinarian makes me the "bad guy" in the eyes of my children.

Always Sometimes Seldom Never

I'd rather not talk about who's the leader in our home.

Always Sometimes Seldom Never

Some tasks around the house are definitely feminine, others definitely masculine.

Always Sometimes Seldom Never

Start Making Some Changes—in Yourself

Note that in 1 Peter 3:8,9 Peter points out the characteristics that are part of the marriage relationship when husband and wife are living by God's plan. Peter says, "You should be like one big happy family, full of sympathy toward each other, loving one another with tender hearts and humble minds."

Read these guidelines from 1 Peter with yourself in mind. Compare Peter's instructions for each marriage partner with what is going on in your marriage now. Is the wife respectful and submissive to the husband's views? Is the husband careful, strong, thoughtful and loving, protecting his wife from the pressures and buffeting of life? Just who is making the decisions? Is one spouse making them all, without really trying to communicate or share ideas?

Perhaps you see changes that need to be made. Perhaps it is easier to see changes your mate should be making. But how can you begin?

Don't begin with your mate.

Begin with yourself.

"Before you can have any hope of changing your partner, you will need to make some very crucial changes.

"Since criticizing and suggesting changes only increase the problem by decreasing understanding, love and acceptance between you, discard it. Stop it all. Determine to give the most wholehearted love and acceptance possible—without conditions. But then, if you can't criticize and correct the other, how will you proceed?

"By being a different sort of person. Instead of accepting with spoken or unspoken reservations, genuinely accept him or her as you promised in that long ago ceremony. Vows are nothing if they do not become a way of life—a daily commitment of life. And your vows were not to educate, reform and restructure your mate, but to love. The crucial commitment of marriage is the pledge to be the right mate to the other person. Forget whether you 'found the right mate.'

Who could know? Who could say? And so what if you did or didn't discover just-the-very-very-right-and-perfect-person-for-grand-old-you?

"What kind of person are you being? Are you committed to being the right mate here and now? Do that, be that, and you'll make a change for the better in both of you. Almost instantly."(5)

WHAT'S YOUR PLAN?

If you are studying this book with your spouse, best results can be obtained if you complete the following material individually and then discuss your answers together. As you compare ideas, feelings and attitudes you will achieve new levels of communication and understanding in your marriage.

Set aside time this week to study 1 Peter 3:1-9. Read the passage two or three times and note words or phrases that seem especially significant to you. Then complete the following in a personal notebook:

1. Describe the behavior or attitude that you want to change (for example: wanting to have the last word, wanting to make all or most of the major decisions, feeling your way is really best, etc.).

2. List several very personal reasons for giving up this behavior or attitude. What will changing this mean to you personally?

3. Motivation to change is very important. From your reasons for giving up the behavior or attitude select the *most important reason.* Write it down.

4. Begin to think about *how* you should change your behavior if you wish to succeed. Write these ideas down.

5. Adopt a positive attitude. What has been your attitude toward changing this in the past? Describe. How will you maintain your new attitude? Write it down.

6. Many times when you eliminate a behavior or attitude that you dislike a vacuum or void will remain. Frequently a person prefers the bad or poor behavior to this emptiness so he reverts back to the previous pattern. In order for this *not* to happen decide what *positive behavior* you want to substitute in place of the negative one you are giving up. Describe this positive behavior attitude.

7. Search for Scriptures that will help you in this problem area and your determination to change. Read Ephesians 4:31,32. Choose any word, phrase or thought that encourages you or gives you a specific guideline. For encouragement read Philippians 4:13,19.

CHAPTER 4

what was that I never heard you say?

As you read this chapter, you will discover . . .

. . . why communication can be such a problem

. . . that communication is more than talking

. . . listening is an essential part of building strong lines of communication in a marriage

. . . the valuable Biblical guidelines for communicating

. . . how husbands and wives frustrate each other (and how to avoid it)

. . . specific ways you can improve your communication skills.

"But why can't we communicate?"

That's a familiar question, especially for a lot of husbands and wives. But before asking "Why no communication?" take time to ask yourself, "What does the word communication mean to me?"

WHAT DO YOU THINK? #10

My definition of communication is . . .

Communication Is a Process

There are many definitions of communication. One very good and simple definition is that communication is a process (either verbal or nonverbal) of sharing information with another person in such a way that he understands what you are saying. *Talking* and *listening* and *understanding* are all involved in the process of communication.

One of the key problems in communicating is making yourself understood. (See cartoon this page.) We often *do* think we understand what our mate is saying, but often what we heard is not what he or she means at all. In fact, our spouses may not be sure they themselves know what they mean in the first place!

I KNOW YOU BELIEVE YOU UNDERSTAND WHAT YOU THINK I SAID, BUT I'M NOT SURE YOU REALIZE THAT WHAT YOU HEARD IS NOT WHAT I MEANT.

When you stop to think about all that's involved in getting your message across it's apparent why misunderstandings often occur. Communication specialists point out that when you talk with another person there are actually six messages that can come through.

1. What you mean to say.
2. What you actually say.
3. What the other person hears.
4. What the other person thinks he hears.
5. What the other person says about what you said.
6. What you think the other person said about what you said.

Discouraging? Rather. But it does illustrate why communication is often hard work. We want the other person not only to listen, but to understand what we mean. The old proverb, "Say what you mean and mean what you say," is a worthy goal, but not an easy one to achieve.

WHAT DO YOU THINK? #11

Here are three questions to help you think about yourself as a communicator.

1. Is communicating with your spouse difficult for you?

Often Sometimes Almost never

2. Does your mate seem to have difficulty understanding what you mean?

Often Sometimes Almost never

3. What do you think your mate would say about your ability to communicate?

Great So-so Impossible

To Communicate—Listen More, Talk Less

In his book *Herein Is Love,* Reuel Howe says, "If there is any indispensable insight with which a young married couple should begin their life together, it is that they should try to keep open, at all cost, the lines of communication between them."(1)

Unfortunately, it is not uncommon for communication lines to be down. Sometimes these breaks in communication are due to the husband and/or wife not being willing or able to talk about what's happening in his or her life. But just as often it is the result of marriage partners not really listening when the other talks. There cannot be strong lines of communication without real listening.

Someone has suggested that listening intently with one's mouth shut is a basic communication skill needed in marriages. Think about your own communication pattern. Do you listen? How much of what is said do you hear? It has been estimated that usually a person hears only about 20 percent of what is said. What is involved in effective listening?

Listening effectively means that when someone is talking you are not thinking about what you are going to say when the other person stops. Instead, you are totally tuned in to what the other person is saying. As Paul Tournier says, "How beautiful, how grand and liberating this experience is, when people learn to help each other. It is impossible to overemphasize the immense need humans have to be really listened to."

Listening is more than politely waiting for your turn to speak. It is more than hearing words. Real listening is receiving and accepting the message as it is sent—seeking to understand what the other person really means. When this happens you can go further than saying, "I hear you." You can say, "I hear what you mean."

While listening is generally regarded as a passive part of communication, this is not true. Sensitive listening is reaching out to the other person, actively caring about what he says and what he wants to say.

In his book *After You've Said I Do,* Dwight Small points out that listening does not come naturally nor does it come easily to most people. Listening is not our natural preference. Most people prefer to be the one speaking. We like to express our ideas. We feel more comfortable identifying our position, asserting our opinions and feelings. Actually, most people do not want to hear as much as they want to speak and to be heard. Because of this we concentrate more on getting our word into the conversation, rather than giving full attention to what the other person is saying. Also, all too often we filter the other person's remarks through our own opinions and our own needs.

For example, a wife mentions that she's tired of housework. Her husband hears what she says, but the message he receives is that she is unhappy because he isn't providing her with household help like her mother has. That's not what the wife had in mind, but it is what the husband heard. Ever since they were married it has bothered him that he cannot provide help for the home like his wife's father does. It is easy to see how the message came through differently than the wife intended. Filtered messages are seldom accurate and cause much misunderstanding.(2)

When both husband and wife recognize the importance of listening objectively, and giving each other full attention, they are taking big steps toward building strong lines of communication.

WHAT DO YOU THINK? #12

How would you describe yourself as a listener?

1. As your mate talks to you, do you find it difficult to

keep your mind from wandering to other things?

Yes No Sometimes

2. When your mate talks, do you go beyond the facts being discussed and try to sense how he or she is feeling about the matter?

Yes No Sometimes

3. Do certain things or phrases your mate says prejudice you so that you cannot objectively listen to what is being said?

Yes No Sometimes

4. When you are puzzled or annoyed by what your mate says, do you try to get the question straightened out as soon as possible?

Yes No Sometimes

5. If you feel it would take too much time and effort to understand something, do you go out of your way to avoid hearing about it?

Yes No Sometimes

6. When your mate talks to you do you try to make him or her think you are paying attention when you are not?

Yes No Sometimes

7. When you are listening to the other person are you easily distracted by outside sights and sounds (such as the TV set)?

Yes No Sometimes

Look back over your answers. Do they give you clues for improving your listening attitudes and skills?

WE FILTER WHAT WE HEAR THROUGH OUR FEELINGS

The Bible Speaks of Word Power

Children attending school soon learn to chant the sing-song poem, "Sticks and stones may break my bones, but words will never hurt me." But experience quickly teaches that this is untrue. Words can and do hurt a person. The Bible recognizes this and talks about word power in both the Old and New Testaments.

Proverbs 18:21 states what many have discovered: *Death and life are in the power of the tongue* (*NASB*). Proverbs 26:22 also speaks of how words really get to a person: *The words of a whisperer . . . go down to the innermost parts of the body (NASB).* This was what Job was experiencing when he cried in frustration, *How long will you torment me, and crush me with words?* (*NASB*). or as *The Living Bible* puts it, *How long are you going to trouble me, and try to break me with your words?* (Job 19:2).

James 3:2-10 talks about the power of words and why it is

so important to control the tongue. Surely here are key ideas for improving communications in a marriage:

If anyone can control his tongue, it proves that he has perfect control over himself in every other way. We can make a large horse turn around and go wherever we want by means of a small bit in his mouth.

And a tiny rudder makes a huge ship turn wherever the pilot wants it to go, even though the winds are strong.

So also the tongue is a small thing, but what enormous damage it can do. A great forest can be set on fire by one tiny spark. And the tongue is a flame of fire. It is full of wickedness, and poisons every part of the body. And the tongue is set on fire by hell itself, and can turn our whole lives into a blazing flame of destruction and disaster.

Men have trained, or can train, every kind of animal or bird that lives and every kind of reptile and fish, but no human being can tame the tongue. It is always ready to pour out its deadly poison. Sometimes it praises our heavenly Father, and sometimes it breaks out into curses against men who are made like God. And so blessing and cursing come pouring out of the same mouth. Dear brothers, surely this is not right! (TLB).

James compares the power of the tongue to the rudder of a ship, as far as power is concerned. Comparatively speaking, a rudder is a small part of the ship, yet it can turn the ship in any direction and control its destiny. What husbands and wives say to one another can turn their marriage in different directions (and in some cases cause them to wind up going in a vicious circle).

Continuing to emphasize the tongue's potency, James compares it to a flame of fire. Great forests can be leveled by one tiny spark. In the same way, a marriage can be damaged and in some cases even "set on fire" by one remark, or (more typically) by continually chopping and snipping away at each other.

Words do spread like fire. Did you ever try to stop a rumor? Did you ever attempt to squelch an unkind story once it was told? Impossible! Who can unsay words or wipe out what has been heard?

James continues to bear down on the difficulty in controlling the tongue when he writes that man's ingenuity has succeeded in taming almost every kind of living creature; yet he has failed in taming his own tongue! According to the dictionary "to tame" means "to control" and "to render useful and beneficial." Man has not been able to do that with his tongue on any widespread basis.

Each person must be responsible for his own tongue-training program. Controlling the tongue needs to be a continuing aim for each husband and wife because *everything* that is said either helps . . . or hinders; heals . . . or scars; builds up . . . or tears down.

According to Scripture, the husband or wife who just blurts out whatever he or she is thinking or feeling without considering the consequences is in a bad way indeed: *Do you see a man who is hasty in his words? There is more hope for a fool than for him* (Pro. 29:20, *NASB*).

First Peter 3:10 sums it up nicely: *If you want a happy, good life, keep control of your tongue, and guard your lips . . . (TLB).* To control your tongue is not easy to accomplish in your own strength, but the Christian who depends on the Holy Spirit for teaching and guidance has help and strength far beyond his own. Remember how good it feels when you have a comfortable, "building-up" kind of conversation with your spouse? You concentrate on choosing words that are kind and appropriate for the time and purpose. And your mate does the same. And the result is that you build up each other and create a rewarding situation for yourself. Proverbs 25:11 describes the beauty of such a moment: *A word fitly spoken is like apples of gold in a setting of silver* (*RSV*). Or as Proverbs 15:23 says, *How wonderful . . . to say the right thing at the right time (TLB).*

The Bible also gives tips on how to listen. The ability to use words well isn't all that is required to make a person an effective communicator. An anonymous wit once pointed out that the Lord created man with one mouth and two ears and perhaps this is an indication of how much talking and how much listening we should do!

Proverbs 18:13 gives an important reason for listening carefully: *He who gives an answer before he hears, it is folly and shame to him (NASB).* According to Scripture, listening means taking time to know what the situation is before jumping to conclusions (and going off with your tongue half-cocked).

In James 1:19 the Christian is told to *be quick to hear* or as it is put in the *Amplified* version: *be a ready listener.* Too many of us are ready talkers, but we have little or no desire to listen. Yet, one of the keys to a successful marriage is *wanting* to hear your mate out. You must make the effort to listen.

To be sure, listening takes effort but at the same time it frees us from ourselves and from our own interests and makes it possible for us to take in what the other person has to say. In so many cases, communication breaks down in a marriage because each partner is so wrapped up and enslaved by his own interests and ideas that he fails to try to understand his mate. And of course the result is that his mate does not understand him. But when husband and wife start to listen to one another an amazing thing happens: they start to feel understood by each other.

One of the difficulties in listening is that one partner tries to second guess the other. It is easy to think that you know what your partner is going to say, so you cut your partner off and finish the sentence or interrupt his idea with something that he or she doesn't mean at all. All too often a husband or wife blurts out an opinion that is miles from the wavelength that the other partner is on. This is what the writer of Proverbs had in mind when he said: *What a shame—yes, how stupid—to decide before knowing the facts!* (Prov. 18:13, *TLB*).

To Understand—Communicate!

In his book, *The Art of Understanding Your Mate,* Cecil Osborne suggests several ways in which men and women frustrate one another in the marriage relationship. For example, women frustrate their husbands by "taking over" and assuming dominance, or by tending to become emotional in a discussion. Men are also frustrated when women refuse to abandon the romantic dreams of girlhood.

On the other hand, men frustrate their wives by failing to understand the somewhat volatile emotions of their wives. Women often have strong mood swings and may be depressed or made happy by events that do not deeply affect a man. Women are also frustrated by men failing to understand that "little things" as he sees them, are often "big things" to her. For instance, outside activities of the husband, like sports, hobbies and even work, are frequently sources of frustration to the wife.

But, as Osborne points out, the major source of frustration for wives by their husbands is *that men do not communicate with* or *listen to their wives.* And to be fair, this can be the case with wives as well.

An additional source of frustration is that all too often husbands and wives concentrate on the talking aspect of communication because they are overly concerned about getting their ideas across. In doing this they fail to listen to the other party. When this happens husbands and wives have no real idea of what the other is really thinking or feeling. They may talk, but do they really say anything? Or hear anything? Many conversations are dominated with responses like "unhuh," "Yes," and "I see," and then five minutes later both husband and wife wonder what went on. (3)

Such lack of communication can produce real marriage problems. In fact, many marriage counselors say that the number one problem in marriage is poor communication.

Marriage is an intimate relationship built on mutual understanding, but in order to truly understand another person you must be able to communicate with him. A husband and wife can know a great deal *about* each other without really knowing one another. Communication is the process that allows people to know each other, to relate to one another, to understand the true meaning of the other person's life.

WHAT'S YOUR PLAN?

If you are studying this book with your spouse, best results can be obtained if you complete the following material individually and then discuss your answers together. As you compare ideas, feelings and attitudes you will achieve new levels of communication and understanding in your marriage.

1. Circle the phrase that you feel describes the quality of communication in your marriage:

a. needs no improvement
b. highly effective
c. satisfactory
d. inconsistent
e. superficial
f. frustrating
g. highly inadequate

Now go back and underline the phrase which you think your spouse would choose.

2. List three things *you* can do to improve communication between yourself and your spouse. "I plan to improve our communication by:

a.

b.

c.

I will start doing these three things *(date)* ___________
(time) ______________________"

3. Make an "appointment" with your mate when you can sit down (perhaps over a cup of coffee) and plan together how you can improve your communication.
(date) ______________ *(time)* ______________

As you do your planning together be sure to cover the four following points:

a. Share and discuss your responses to question 1 on the quality of communication in your marriage.

b. Also share your responses to question 2 on how you plan to improve communication. Ask your mate's opinion to see if he or she feels if your suggestion will actually improve communication. If not, work out alternate ideas that both of you approve of.

c. Commit yourself to following your plans for improving communication and stick to it for at least one week.

d. Set a date for one week from now to get together again and evaluate how successful your plan has been. If necessary, revise your plan at that time and repeat the process until you both feel that communication between you is improving.

CHAPTER 5

why can't we talk about it?

As you read this chapter, you will discover . . .

. . . four hangups that keep people from communicating

. . . that we communicate at five different levels, from shallow clichés to deep honest openness

. . . that Scripture teaches a definite relationship between self-acceptance (through God's love) and the willingness to accept and communicate with others

. . . that communication with God is vital to communication with each other

. . . how to plan specific ways to improve communication with God and each other.

"But I just don't want to talk about it!" Ever hear that from the other half? Ever use it yourself when you are out of patience (or ideas) about what to say next?

There are basic reasons why a lot of us can't get through or can't be reached. And there are basic Scriptural principles which will help us communicate more effectively.

Reasons for Not Communicating

Why is it that some people do not communicate? They often have basic hangups or weaknesses such as these:

1. A few people do not have the ability to talk with another person. They have never learned how to share openly with someone else and they have difficulty forming the words.

2. Others are fearful of exposing what they feel or think. They do not want to run the risk of being rejected or hurt if someone else disagrees with them. This is a protective device. The ability to communicate is not lost when married couples grow apart. It is the desire to communicate that undergoes change. When one or the other no longer wants to be understood or to be understanding, then distance will develop.

3. Others have the attitude that talking won't do any good, so why bother? They are unable to get through to the other person so they stop trying.

4. Some people do not believe that they as a person have anything to offer. They do not think that their ideas are worthwhile. They have what is called a poor self-image and, as a result, they withhold their comments and personal feelings. They have difficulty accepting themselves.

There are times when it is easy to identify the obstacles to good communication. Other times there is a complex mixture of reasons that is hard to pin down. Think back to a situation when you and your spouse couldn't communicate. What was the *real* reason?

WHAT DO YOU THINK? #13

1. Which reason for not communicating applies to you?
   - ☐ can't talk to others
   - ☐ afraid to expose thoughts
   - ☐ feel "why bother?"
   - ☐ ideas not worthwhile

2. Which reason for not communicating applies to your mate?
   - ☐ can't talk to others
   - ☐ afraid to expose thoughts
   - ☐ feel "why bother?"
   - ☐ ideas not worthwhile

3. Maybe you have another reason for not wanting to communicate. If so, describe it in ten words or less.

The Five Levels of Communication

In his excellent book, *Why Am I Afraid to Tell You Who I Am?*, John Powell asserts that we communicate on at least five different levels, from shallow clichés to deep personal honesty. Hangups such as fear, apathy or a poor self-image keep us at the shallow level, but if we can be freed from our weaknesses, we can move to the deeper, more meaningful level.

Powell's five levels of communication include:

Level Five: Cliché Conversation. This type of talk is very safe. We use words such as "How are you?" "How is your family?" "Where have you been?" "I like your suit." In this type of conversation there is no personal sharing. Each person remains safely behind his screen.

Level Four: Reporting the Facts About Others. In this kind of conversation we are content to tell others what someone else has said, but we offer no personal commentary on these facts. We just report the facts like the five o'clock news each day. We share gossip and little narrations but we do not commit ourselves as to how we feel about it.

Level Three: My Ideas and Judgments. This is where some real communication begins. The person is willing to step out of his solitary confinement and risk telling some of his ideas and decisions. He is still cautious, however, and if he senses that what he is saying is not being accepted he will retreat.

Level Two: My Feelings or Emotions. Now the person shares how he feels about facts, ideas and judgments. The feelings underneath these areas are revealed. If a person is to really share himself with another individual he must get to the level of sharing his feelings.

Level One: Complete Emotional and Personal Truthful Communication. All deep relationships, especially marriage relationships, *must* be based on absolute openness and honesty. This may be difficult to achieve because it involves a risk—the risk of being rejected because of our honesty, but it is vital for relationships to grow in marriage. There will be times when this type of communication is achieved and other times when the communication is not as complete as it could be. (1)

These are five suggested levels of communication. Only you know at what level communication is occurring in your marriage. But ask yourself, "What *is* our communication like? On which level are we? How can we move toward Level One in our relationship?"

How are You?
I'M FINE.
LEVEL 5
CLICHÉS
DID YOU HEAR about Grace and Howard? SHE'S Pregnant again.
That reminds me... SHEBA is Going to Have Pups again.
LEVEL 4
Reporting the facts
WOMAN'S PLACE is in the HOME... WHO'LL DO the HOUSE WORK?
But WHY SHOULD'NT I take a Part-TIME JOB? WE NEED the MONEY.
LEVEL 3
IDEAS and JUDGMENTS
I JUST CAN'T TAKE another LONG TRIP WITH the KIDS IN THAT Car. WE'VE GOT TO GET SOMETHING BIGGER OR I'LL GO CRAZY!
HOW DO WE HANDLE PAYMENTS? IF the BILLS GET ANY BIGGER... I'LL Go Crazy!
LEVEL 2
FEELINGS and EMOTIONS
I DON'T KNOW IF I REALLY WANT that NEW JOB. I'M NOT Sure I'VE GOT WHAT it takes to BE a Manager.
You're a Terrific SALESMAN... MAYBE THAT'S WHAT You SHOULD CONTINUE To DO.
LEVEL 1
OPEN, Truthful COMMUNICATION
WE COMMUNICATE at DIFFERENT LEVELS

WHAT DO YOU THINK? #14

1. Write down subjects or topics which you discuss with your spouse at the Level One stage of communication—complete emotional and personal truthful communication:

2. Now write down subjects or topics you do not discuss at Level One:

3. What prevents you from communicating on certain subjects at Level One?

4. What do you think can be done about this? List what you can do to help your partner share more deeply with you.

What About Communication with God?

We have been talking about communication especially as it pertains to husband and wife. But what about our communication with God? Are we open in the presence of God or do we use Level Four or Five communication there? Do we share ourselves with Him? Do we do all the talking or do we sit and listen?

In Christian marriage we realize that there are three people involved—God, husband and wife. As you see on the diagram we have a triangle with God as the top or the center. You also see the word communication between each member here. If there is a breakdown in communication between one member and God this will affect the communication between that person and his mate. If there is a break-

KEEP ALL THE LINES OPEN

down in communication between this person and his mate this will affect his communication between himself and God! The communication lines between God and your mate must be open and you must work on keeping these open at all times. One author has suggested that "Lines open to God invariably open to one another, for a person cannot be genuinely open to God and closed to his mate. . . . God fulfills His design for Christian marriage when lines of communication are first opened to Him." (2)

What is it that really frees a person to open his life to another, to reach out to share and to love another person? Before we can love someone, we must have had two basic experiences in our life. First of all, we must have experienced love from someone else and then we must also love ourselves. But what if we grew up never having experienced true unconditional love that is necessary for us to begin loving ourselves? How can one begin to love others and himself when he's an adult? Is it really possible or are we just fooling ourselves? We find that it is possible to experience this unconditional love—from Jesus Christ! Often called the apostle of love, John puts it this way:

9. *By this the love of God was manifested in us, that God has sent His only begotten Son into the world so that we might live through Him.*

10. *In this is love, not that we loved God, but that He loved us and sent His Son to be the propitiation for our sins.*

11. *Beloved, if God so loved us, we also ought to love one another.*

18. *There is no fear in love; but perfect love casts out fear. . . .*

19. *We love, because He first loved us* (1 John 4:9-11,18, 19, *NASB*).

The ability to love yourself and other people is the result of God reaching out and loving you first. When you accept God's forgiveness and acceptance you experience His love. But for many people, right here is where the "catch" comes in. God doesn't cause the problem, we Christians do. Deep down, we really don't believe God accepts us—and the result is that we really don't accept ourselves.

But if Scripture plainly says that God forgives and accepts you, why go on rejecting yourself? Why reject what God has accepted? And not only has God accepted you, but He *accepts you unconditionally*. God attaches no strings to your relationship with Him, so why should you? Why not drop your guard as far as God is concerned? Relax in His presence and your confidence in yourself—as well as in Him—will grow.

As John points out. *There is no fear in love; but perfect love casts out fear* . . . (1 John 4:18, *NASB*). So, let it happen. Let God love you His way—with no conditions, no improvements on your part to make yourself "worthy" of God's love. If you try to "shape up" for God and be "worth loving," you play the same game with Him that you play with others—especially your mate. You set a standard of what you think is lovable. When you don't reach it, or your mate doesn't reach it, you freeze, clutch, or blow up. Fear casts out, or suppresses, the love you want to have for yourself and others.

WHAT DO YOU THINK? #15

Analyze just how much you accept what God has done for you and how He feels about you by completing the following multiple choice statements. Don't choose answers because they look "right." Instead choose answers that really match your true feelings.

1. I think of God as
   - ☐ a distant power
   - ☐ my friend
   - ☐ my policeman
   - ☐ my ______________________________

2. When I pray I feel

- ☐ relaxed and close to God
- ☐ strained and uncertain
- ☐ afraid God is displeased with me
- ☐ ____________________

3. As a Christian I

- ☐ try to do better so I will deserve God's love
- ☐ feel God can't love me the way I act
- ☐ feel unhappy because I belong to God's family
- ☐ ____________________

4. Describe a lovable person in twenty-five words or less. How would God describe a lovable person? How would He describe an unlovable person?

WE COMMUNICATE
WE ACCEPT OTHERS
WE ACCEPT OURSELVES
CHRIST HAS ACCEPTED US AND WE ACCEPT HIS LOVE
CHRIST HAS ACCEPTED US AND WE ACCEPT HIS LOVE
WE ACCEPT OURSELVES
WE ACCEPT OTHERS
WE COMMUNICATE

Doorways to Communication

As you open up to God, you will discover new ability to open up to others. You will be able to communicate at those deeper levels described earlier in this chapter. It works like this:

1. Christ accepts us.
2. We accept Christ's love.
3. We accept ourselves.
4. We accept others.
5. We communicate! (See cartoon.)

Christ's love and acceptance of us gives us the confidence to share ourselves with others. He accepts us with our failures and defects and sees the great potential that lies within us. This potential can now be developed because Christ is in us. Because God accepts us, we can learn to accept ourselves. When we accept ourselves and develop a better self-image, we learn to accept others which leads to a willingness to communicate with those around us. Jesus Christ provides the way for a person to move to the first level of communication!

WHAT'S YOUR PLAN?

If you are studying this book together, best results can be obtained if you complete the following material individually and then discuss your answers with your spouse. As you compare ideas, feelings and attitudes you will achieve new and deeper levels of communication and understanding.

Choose three of the following ideas and try them out during the coming week.

1. Decide if there are areas in your relationship with your spouse that could be improved if you would be willing to share how you feel (Level Two communication). Choose one thing that you will talk about with your mate and share your true feelings. Choose a time that's appropriate and

honestly tell him or her that you want to share your feeling about something because you believe it would help you feel better.

2. Decide if there are areas in your relationship with God that would be improved if you were willing to tell Him how you really feel. (He knows anyway!) Take some time alone this week to tell God your true feelings about yourself and how you feel about Him.

3. Discuss with your mate how he or she feels about God. If your feelings do not agree does this mean that God loves either one of you more than the other? Does your faith in God's acceptance of you "just as you are" help you accept your marriage partner just as he or she is? Can you feel comfortable for your mate to have ideas on certain subjects that do not agree with yours?

4. Write a letter to God telling Him how you feel about His acceptance of you. For ideas read Psalm 103.

5. List ways that you protect yourself or cut yourself off from communicating with your mate. Your list may include things like: reading at mealtime; ironing or doing some task that gives me a degree of privacy; turning on TV rather than continue a conversation; taking a bath so your mate will be asleep when you go to bed; etc., etc. At the end of the week decide which barriers you want to "tear down."

6. Plan a time when you can spend some time with your husband or wife in a relaxed situation (when the children are asleep or with a sitter, for example). It should be a time when you are not in a hurry, a time you can enjoy. Perhaps you will want to take a walk, read aloud to each other or share a snack or just talk about hopes and plans for the future.

7. Plan for one way that you really want to begin to communicate on "Level One" with your husband or wife. Think through what it would really mean to talk about a certain area of your relationship with complete emotional and personal truthfulness. Will talk be enough? What else will you have to do to prepare your husband or wife for your openness? Are there things you can do to build a credibility bridge that will make your openness meaningful and acceptable?

CHAPTER 6

is anger always a "No-No"?

As you read this chapter, you will discover . . .

. . . how anger blocks communication

. . . what anger is

. . . why people get angry

. . . what Scripture says about being angry

. . . typical reactions to anger

. . . how you respond to anger and how you can make needed changes in your attitude toward anger.

Most couples want to communicate with one another. Communication is vitally important when one or both of the partners is angry. Yet anger is one of the main causes of the breakdown of communication in marriage.

Have you ever tried to define the feeling of anger or hostility? Perhaps the simplest definition is a *strong emotion of displeasure*. Emotions generate energy within us. Anger generates energy which impels us to hurt or destroy that which angers us. Anger is the natural, reflexive result of frustration—our reaction to having a goal blocked.

WHAT DO YOU THINK? #16

What is your definition of anger? Do you agree with the definition given above? Why? Why not?

Positive and Negative Points on Anger

Too often we think of anger negatively. But anger also has its positive points. For example, one of our built-in goals is survival. When it appears that that goal is threatened (or may not be reached), the frustration resulting from the blocked goal makes us angry. This emotion can spur us on to almost impossible feats in order to survive.

. . . *Let justice roll down like waters and righteousness like an ever-flowing stream,* God said through Amos the prophet (Amos 5:24, *NASB*). Many of us desire to see justice and righteousness prevail. When this goal is not reached we become angry. And that is a good thing. When we see injustices around us—other people being hurt or taken advantage of—or when we see suffering we become angry because these conditions should not be so! The energy produced by this anger can motivate us to correct the injustices.

Of course, we do not always become angry for such noble reasons. Often our anger results from concern for ourselves —we are selfish. We do not get our own way and we are frustrated and become angry. We make plans, our mate does not agree with them and refuses to cooperate and we become angry.

"But I've already made reservations at the mountain resort," he states.

"You know how my allergy reacts to all that pollen," she retorts. "I want to go to the beach."

"Yeah, but I *always* get sunburned at the beach. Why can't you take your allergy pills?" he questions.

"For the same reason you don't use suntan lotion," she jabs.

And so it goes. Anger can result from the frustration of not getting your own way. Our unconscious goal is to have and do what we want when we want it. Usually anger stemming from this blocked goal strains our relationship with our spouse.

The prophet Jeremiah observed that *"the heart is the most deceitful thing there is, and desperately wicked"* (Jer. 17:9, *TLB*). We often fail to know when we are angry because we hide it behind other reactions. Our anger often conceals itself behind a cloak of resentment, aggression, frustration, hate, fury, indignation, outrage, wrath, antagonism, crossness, hostility, bitterness, destructiveness, spite, rancor, ferocity, scorn, disdain, enmity, malevolence and defiance. Regardless of how we describe it, when we get down to cases we are simply angry.

Our vocabulary is also rich in describing other people who are angry. We call people mad, bitter, frustrated, griped, fed up, sore, excited, seething, annoyed, troubled, antagonistic or antagonized, exasperated, vexed, indignant, furious, provoked, hurt, irked, irritated, sick, cross, hostile, ferocious, savage, deadly, dangerous, and on the offense.

Anger often produces behavior which prevents communication between husband and wife. We describe such communication-shattering behavior as: to hate, wound, damage, annihilate, despise, scorn, disdain, loathe, vilify, curse, despoil, ruin, demolish, abhor, abominate, desolate, ridicule, tease, kid, get even, laugh at, humiliate, goad, shame, criticize, cut, take out spite on, rail at, scold, bawl out, humble, irritate, beat up, take for a ride, ostracize, fight, beat, vanquish, compete with, brutalize, crush, offend and bully. When we find our feelings or actions described by these terms we should stop kidding ourselves. We are angry. Face that fact so that it can be dealt with.

Some Biblical Thoughts on Anger

What does the Bible say about anger in the lives of men? The Bible gives us several directives and thoughts about this emotion called anger.

The Bible says to put some kinds of anger away.

Let all bitterness and indignation and wrath (passion, rage, bad temper) and resentment (anger, animosity) and quarreling (brawling, clamor, contention) and slander (evil-speaking, abusive or blasphemous language) be banished from you, with all malice (spite, ill will or baseness of any kind) (Eph. 4:31, *Amplified*).

In this verse, Paul is referring to anger as a turbulent emotion, the boiling agitation of the feelings. It is passion boiling up within us.

The Christian is also to put away the anger that is abiding and habitual, the kind of anger which seeks revenge:

But now put away and rid yourselves completely of all these things: anger, rage, bad feeling toward others, curses and slander and foulmouthed abuse and shameful utterances from your lips! (Col. 3:8, *Amplified*).

Scripture teaches us not to provoke others to anger:

The terror of a king is as the roaring of a lion; whoever provokes him to anger or angers himself against him sins against his own life (Prov. 20:2, *Amplified*).

Fathers, do not provoke or irritate or fret your children—do not be hard on them or harass them; lest they become discouraged and sullen and morose and feel inferior and frustrated; do not break their spirit (Col. 3:21, *Amplified*). (See also Eph. 6:4.)

The Bible directs us to be "slow to anger" (that is, to control our anger) and to be careful of close association with others who are constantly angry or hostile.

He who is slow to anger is better than the mighty, and he who rules his own spirit than he who takes a city (Prov. 16:32, *Amplified*).

A hot-tempered man stirs up strife, but the slow to anger pacifies contention (Prov. 15:18, *NASB*).

Make no friendships with a man given to anger, and with a wrathful man do not associate, lest you learn his ways and get yourself into a snare (Prov. 22:24,25, *Amplified*).

Scripture also speaks of "justified anger." An example of justified anger is found in the life of the Lord Jesus:

And He glanced around at them with vexation and anger, grieved at the hardening of their hearts, and said to the man, Hold out your hand. He held it out, and his hand was (completely) restored (Mark 3:5, *Amplified*).

In Ephesians 4:26 the apostle Paul speaks of two different kinds of anger and how to deal with both:

When angry, do not sin; do not ever let your wrath—your exasperation, your fury or indignation—last until the sun goes down (Eph. 4:26, *Amplified*).

In the phrase, "When angry, do not sin," Paul is describing the kind of anger that is an abiding, settled attitude against sin and sinful things. You are aware that you are angry and you are in control of your anger. In this verse, God is actually instructing us to be angry—but about the right thing! Anger is an emotion created by God; He created us as emotional beings. The phrase, "do not sin," is a check against going too far. The kind of anger that is justified because it is against sin and sinful things and fully under your control is the kind of anger that has God's approval.

In the phrase, *"Do not ever let your wrath . . . last until the sun goes down,"* Paul has another meaning. Here he links anger to irritation, exasperation and embitterment. As earlier mentioned in Ephesians 4:31 and Colossians 3:8, we are supposed to put this kind of anger away. If we do get angry in this negative sense, we should deal with it quickly, "before sundown." Scripture counsels us to never take irritation or embitterment to bed. If we do we are sure to lose sleep (not to mention peace, friends and even our health).

WHAT DO YOU THINK? #17

1. Using the previous Biblical descriptions of anger, describe the kind of anger that you usually experience.

How do you express this anger?

2. Describe the kind of anger your spouse seems to usually experience.

How does your spouse usually express this anger?

3. What can a person do to make himself "slow to anger"?

4. Describe how a person can "be angry and sin not."

How We Respond to Anger

How do people react when they are angry—especially in the husband-wife relationship? What choices do they seem to make almost automatically? For most of us there are at least four basic reactions that we have to anger.

1. *We suppress anger.* To suppress anger is like building a fence around it. You recognize you are angry and consciously try to keep your anger under control instead of letting your bad feelings spill out in uncontrolled actions or words.

Suppressing anger is what the writer of Proverbs had in mind when he said: *A [self-confident] fool utters all his anger, but a wise man keeps it back and stills it* (Prov. 29:11, *Amplified*). The same idea is found in Proverbs 14:29: *A wise man controls his temper. He knows that anger causes mistakes (TLB).*

In the New Testament James gives good advice on how

to suppress anger: . . . *let every one be quick to hear, slow to speak and slow to anger* (Jas. 1:19, *NASB*). To "be quick to hear" is another way to say, "listen carefully." If you can listen to what's going on and hold back long enough to think about what you are going to say, you can usually control your anger in a healthy way. As Dr. William Menninger says, "Do not talk when angry but after you have calmed down." (1)

It is important, however, to eventually talk about your anger. Somewhere, somehow the anger has to be recognized and released in a healthy manner. Otherwise your storage apparatus will begin to overflow at the wrong time and the wrong place.

2. *We express anger.* The opposite reaction to suppressing anger is to express it. Anger is a strong emotion and it needs expression in some way. Some people go so far as to advocate cutting loose and expressing exactly how you feel, when you feel it, no matter how much damage you do.

EXPRESS ANGER-LET IT ALL HANG OUT

Granted, expressing anger with violent passion, yelling, sharp words and high emotions does get results but the results are usually not too positive. We like to say that we feel better because we "got it off our chest," but chances are, neither you nor the people you blast really profit from uncontrolled expressions of anger. Waiting until you've cooled off is better for all concerned. Reread Proverbs 29:11 and Proverbs 14:29. In most cases Solomon makes it clear that a fool goes off half-cocked with uncontrolled anger while the wise man holds on to his temper.

This doesn't mean that you don't express anger in some way. Some people learn to express their anger by redirecting it. They get busy doing something that gives them time to cool off as they use up some of the emotional energy they've generated by becoming angry. Some people go out into the yard and cut the grass or dig in the garden. Some walk around the block and others ride a bicycle. Others find it helpful to sit down and write out exactly how they feel.

Scrubbing a floor, washing a car or doing anything that takes physical effort can be a good way of working out the strong, pent-up feelings of anger. Whatever helps you calm down and control your feelings is a good course of action for you as long as it does not hurt others or damage their property.

3. *We repress anger.* The person who represses anger refuses to accept the fact that he is angry. Many Christians practice repression.

As a Christian you may honestly think that because you know Christ you are not supposed to become angry—the anger is not a legitimate emotion for you. Therefore, when angry feelings arise you attempt to ignore them and refuse to accept their presence. Because of what you've been taught in sermons and possibly in things that you have read, you feel that anger is always a sin and therefore off limits for anyone practicing Christian behavior.

But this isn't the case and it isn't what Scripture actually teaches. Anger is a God-given emotion. The Bible doesn't teach us to repress anger but to control it. In a way, we need anger as part of our personality and makeup.

As Dr. J. H. Jowett says, "A life incapabable of anger is destitute of the needful energy for all reform. There is no blaze in it, there is no ministry of purification. . . . We are taught in the New Testament that this power of indignation is begotten by the Holy Spirit. The Holy Spirit makes us capable of healthy heat, and it inspires the fire within us. The Holy Spirit doesn't create a character that is lukewarm, neutral or indifferent." (2)

Ignoring anger and refusing to recognize its presence is NOT HEALTHY. Repressing anger is like taking a wastepaper basket full of paper and putting it in a closet and setting it on fire. True the fire can burn itself out OR it can set the entire house on fire and burn it down. Actually, ulcers, anxiety, headaches or depression are common results of repressing anger.

Dr. David Augsburger observes, "Repressed anger hurts and keeps on hurting. If you always deal with it simply by holding it firmly in check or sweeping it under the rug, without any form of release or healing it can produce rigidity and coldness in personality . . . Or repressed anger may come out indirectly in critical attitudes, scapegoating or irritableness." (3)

John Powell sums it up nicely when he says, "When I repress my emotions my stomach keeps score." (4)

If you are afraid of recognizing anger in your own life remember that God's Word recognizes the presence of anger, and although it gives advice to avoid anger and to control it, the Bible does not say to ignore your angry feelings.

Anger does serve a purpose. God Himself has anger against what is wrong. *For God's [holy] wrath and indignation are revealed from heaven against all ungodliness and unrighteousness of men* (Rom. 1:18, *Amplified*). Mark 3:5 tells about one of the times that Christ was angry, *And He glanced around at them with vexation and anger, grieved at the hardening of their hearts (Amplified).*

As already mentioned, the apostle Paul recognized that anger is a part of life. That's why he wrote: *When angry, do not sin . . .* (Eph. 4:26, *Amplified*). Notice that he did not write, "do not sin by being angry."

The point is this. Admitting the presence of anger is a healthy way to respond to anger in your life. Ignoring anger and repressing your feelings of anger only make matters worse. Getting angry is not necessarily a sin, but repression of anger is always a sin.

Dr. William Menninger writes, "Sometimes we push each other away and the problem between us festers and festers. Just as in surgery, free and adequate drainage is essential if healing is to take place." (5)

Repression of anger is the worst possible response that we can make to being angry. Unfortunately, it is an all too common response among Christians.

4. *We confess anger.* Some people react to anger by recognizing they are getting angry and they can confess it before their feelings get out of control. This is an excellent response to make to your mate when things are getting a little tense. The secret is to confess your anger in a way that your spouse will be able to accept. You might say, "You know, the way the discussion is going I'm starting to get angry. Now I don't want to get angry and I know you don't want me to get angry so perhaps we could stop the discussion, start over and see if I can get my feelings under control."

Whatever you do don't say, "You're making me angry." This puts your spouse at fault and will put him or her on the defensive. *Always recognize that you are responsible for your own emotional reaction toward another person.* Confessing your anger to the other person simply means that you are willing to admit that you have a problem. You might say: "I'm sorry I'm angry. What can I do now so we can work this thing out?"

CONFESS ANGER — GET IT OUT IN THE OPEN.

The Living Bible paraphrase of Ephesians 4:26,27 gives some good clues on responding to anger by confessing it:

If you are angry, don't sin by nursing your grudge. Don't let the sun go down with you still angry—get over it quickly; for when you are angry you give a mighty foothold for the devil (*TLB*).

Paul was well aware that when you nurse a grudge you can grow a consuming hatred. Paul advises the Ephesian Christians (and us) to never nurse a grudge and let anger fester and rage within. To confess anger is to get it out in the open where you can discuss the cause of the trouble.

Confessing anger is a response that is usually more difficult for most of us, because by the time we admit we are angry it has already become obvious to our spouse, or whomever we are angry with, that we are definitely irritated and uptight. The key is to learn how to confess anger in a way that does not make the other person feel that you are angry with him already!

WHAT DO YOU THINK? #18

1. What is your usual response when you get angry?

Suppress   Express   Repress   Confess

2. Do you agree with John Powell when he says, "When I repress my emotions my stomach keeps score"? What are other possible ways that repressed anger seems to affect you? Does it make you irritable? critical? touchy? Would you say that you are aware that you sometimes repress anger and don't want to admit that you are angry?

3. Does confessing anger seem like a real possibility for you? That is, is it something that you do easily or think that you could start doing? What would people say if you were honest and let them know when they were making you angry?

My spouse would say:

My friends would say:

My boss would say:

Make the Most of Your Anger

In his book, *Be All That You Can Be,* David Augsburger suggests the following ways to make the most of anger. First of all a person must understand that "anger is a vital, valid, natural emotion. As an emotion, it is in itself neither right nor wrong. The rightness or wrongness depends on the way it is released and exercised.

"Be angry, but be aware. You are never more vulnerable than when in anger. Self-control is at an all-time low, reason decreases, common sense usually forsakes you.

"Be angry, but be aware that anger quickly turns bitter, it sours into resentment, hatred, malice, and even violence unless it is controlled by love.

"Be angry, but only to be kind. Only when anger is motivated by love of your brother, by love of what is right for people, by what is called from you by love for God, is it constructive, creative anger.

"Make the most of your anger. Turn it from selfish defensiveness to selfless compassion." (6)

WHAT'S YOUR PLAN?

If you are studying this book with your spouse, best results can be obtained if you complete the following material individually and then discuss your answers together. As you compare ideas, feelings and attitudes you will achieve new levels of communication and understanding.

Use the following questionnaire to evaluate your own attitude toward anger—what being angry does to you and what you do to others when you get angry. After each question write in "yes," "no," or a more accurate response (using as few words as possible).

1. Do you have a temper?

2. Do you control it?

3. Do others know when you are angry?

4. Describe how you feel when angry.

5. Does your anger surge up quickly?

6. Do you hold resentments?

7. Does your anger affect you physically?

8. Have you ever hit someone or something?

9. When was the last time?

10. How do you control your anger?

11. Who taught you?

12. Are others afraid of your anger?

13. Are others afraid of your criticism?

14. What causes your anger or criticism?

15. How often do you get angry?

16. What are you dissatisfied with in life?

17. Do you get mad at people or things?

18. What do you do about your anger?

19. How do you handle anger directed toward you?

20. Do you repress your anger?

21. Do you suppress it?

22. Do you express or confess it?

23. Do you know of Scriptures that can help you?

24. Do you regularly memorize Scriptures?

25. Do you openly and honestly pray about your emotions?

26. Do you really expect God to help you change your emotions?

27. Do YOU want to change?

If you are not satisfied with the way you respond to anger, then what are you going to do now to change your attitudes and behavior? Look back over the previous chapter and think of some specific things you can do to change and list them here.

CHAPTER 7

how to handle anger (before it handles you)

As you read this chapter, you will discover . . .

. . . how a critical attitude can communicate anger

. . . the difference between healthy and unhealthy approaches to anger

. . . ten practical principles for dealing constructively with angry feelings

. . . how to use Scriptural guidelines to deal with attitudes of anger, criticism or hostility.

Like it or not, anger is a part of life—including married life. In fact, as the previous chapter points out, anger is an emotion given to man by God Himself. Our problem is that we don't handle anger very well. We tend to become angry for the wrong reason or we tend to express angry feelings in a hurtful or damaging way rather than trying to help others and ourselves.

How Critical Are You?

For example, one "wrong reason" for anger is a critical attitude. The angry, hostile person is almost always a critical person. He attacks other people verbally or subtly. If you constantly dislike what you see in other people you may be this way. When you look for and are overly aware of the faults and weaknesses in others you are too critical and hostile. A person with a critical or hostile disposition is not going to be happy and will alienate those about him.

Are you really critical? Ask yourself these questions: Do you spend more time criticizing people in your mind than looking at their strong points? Do others do things that bother you so much that you feel you have to tell them? Do you talk about others in a derogatory manner behind their back? Do you have standards for others that you can't live up to yourself? Do you pressure others to conform to your standards so you can accept them easier?

These reactions indicate a critical or hostile attitude.

Why are we critical? It gets attention off of us. It may make us feel better at the expense of others. In his *Psychology and Morals,* Dr. J. A. Hadfield writes: "It is literally true that in judging others we are trumpeting abroad our own secret faults. We personalize our unrecognized failings, and hate in others the sins to which we are secretly addicted." He goes on to say that the real reason for our condemnation of certain sins in others is that these same sins are a temptation to ourselves. It is for this very reason that we denounce so vehemently the miserliness, bigotry or cynicism of others. Whatever fault we are most intolerant of in others is likely to be amongst our own besetting sins. "Most of our emotions are directed against ourselves," writes Dr. Hadfield. "Allow any man to give free vent to his feelings and then you may, with perfect safety, turn and say: 'Thou are the man.'" (1)

Whenever we find intense prejudice, intolerance, excessive criticism, and cynicism, we are likely to find projection of our feelings into someone else. We are prone to see in others our own undesirable tendencies.

WHAT DO YOU THINK? #19

1. List the things about which you tend to criticize others:

2. What does this tell you about yourself?

3. How do these attitudes/characteristics compare with the fruit of the Holy Spirit (Gal. 5:22,23)?

4. Stop now and thank God for His forgiveness and ask Him to replace your critical spirit with the fruit of the Holy Spirit. (See Rom. 14:13.)

Healthy and Unhealthy Approaches to Anger

While a critical attitude is a problem for some people, even more of a problem for most of us is expressing angry feelings in a damaging way. Let's suppose you are going through the day and not feeling particularly critical of anyone or anything. But then feelings of anger suddenly (or not so suddenly) well up within. What do you do with them? Are you helpless? Must you blow your top because "that's the way you are"? That's a copout. Anger won't render you "helpless" unless you want it to—unless you secretly enjoy blowing off steam.

The truth is, you *do* have a choice about anger. You can react to anger in one of two ways: healthy or unhealthy.

First take a look at unhealthy reactions that will keep you enslaved, "helplessly" angry:

UNHEALTHY REACTIONS

First, be sure to ignore your emotional reactions. Even though you may be angry with your spouse, tell yourself that your angry feelings have nothing to do with the argument anyway. Even better, if you want to compound the problem, convince yourself that you're not getting upset at

1. IGNORE YOUR FEELINGS
2. LET YOUR STOMACH HANDLE IT.
3. KEEP SAYING... "I'M NOT ANGRY."

UNHEALTHY REACTIONS TO ANGER

4. CONCENTRATE ON "SCORING POINTS" AGAINST YOUR OPPONENT.
5. BLAME YOUR MATE (AS LOUDLY AS YOU CAN).
6. WALK OUT AND FEEL SORRY FOR YOURSELF.

all. So you're perspiring a little—it's probably just warm in the room.

Be sure to keep your anger down in the pit of your stomach, where it won't bother your head. Keep everything on an intellectual level but don't let your spouse know how you feel.

Next, be sure to keep on denying your emotions. Keep telling yourself, "I'm not mad." So your stomach is in a knot and you're perspiring profusely. Keep insisting to your mate that you aren't angry at all. Your mate will believe you (?).

Also, make sure you keep your mind on the argument and how you can get back at your spouse. It's obvious the one with the right moves and bright lines is going to break this whole discussion wide open and come away the winner. And that's what's important, isn't it? Winning the argument? Especially if you are arguing with your spouse, right?

If you really get mad, blame your spouse. Surely it's his (or her) fault! When arguing with your mate, be sure to raise the volume. Find some defect in your spouse and point it out with great precision and accuracy (and a little exaggeration, too, if you can think of it). Very helpful rational things such as, "It's impossible to discuss anything with you. You're just too arrogant. You never (generalizations like this are good, too) listen. You think you're God, don't you?" Naturally, as a good Christian, you will be saying all this to speak the truth in love.

Finally, don't learn from your emotions. Walk out in a huff, take a couple of aspirins and concentrate on how unreasonable your spouse was, is, and always will be! (2)

Obviously, the "unhealthy" reactions listed above are a perfect prescription for disaster in a marriage. Unfortunately, these reactions are all too typical with many husbands and wives. In their book, *Learning for Loving,* Robert McFarland and John Burton point out that "few couples have self-sufficient social skills and emotional maturity to fight constructively for the good of their marriage. We believe consequently that most couples urgently need to develop skills and increase their emotional strength sufficiently to engage themselves in such encounters. We believe that many couples seek to avoid constructive conflict because one or both of them feel that changes will have to take place if adequate communication occurred between them." (3)

But in order to do this couples must be willing to trust each other—to trust one another with their feelings and with their admittals that what they are hearing and feeling hurts or is disturbing. All too often husbands and wives are too proud to admit to each other that they are uncomfortable, angry, hurt, etc. And the result is a stalemate in communication. Dwight Small observes, however, "All communication in an intimate relationship is built upon mutual trust. To confide in another is to be relatively sure, first of all, that a ground of confidence is shared. Mutual trust grows as each partner takes the other into account as a person whose happiness is bound up with his own." (4)

And how about the antidote to all of these unhealthy habits? There is one, if husbands and wives are willing to react to angry feelings in the following *healthy* ways:

HEALTHY REACTIONS

To begin with, be aware of your emotions. Forget the argument momentarily and concentrate on your emotional reactions. What are you feeling? Embarrassment (because her argument sounds better)? Fear ("He's getting nasty—I hope he doesn't hit me")? Superiority ("I'm ahead on points and she knows it")?

Don't be afraid to admit your emotion. Take a good look at yourself and accept the fact that you are angry. If you are honest, you'll admit that it's high voltage anger, not just a "little" irritation or frustration.

Now investigate how the emotion got there. Ask yourself, "Why am I angry? Why is my spouse getting to me like this?" Try to trace the origin of your emotion. You may come up with a glimpse of some hidden inferiority complex which you've never recognized or a fear or a weakness you didn't want to admit to your spouse.

Share your emotion with your spouse. Just present the facts with no interpretations or judgments. Say something to your mate such as, "Let's stop, because I'm saying things I really don't mean and I don't want this to happen." Whatever you do, don't judge or accuse your spouse. It isn't your spouse's fault that you are angry. Don't blame your spouse, even to yourself.

Decide what to do with your emotion. What's the best thing to do next? Perhaps you will want to tell your spouse, "Let's start again. I think I've been too defensive to listen to you. I'd like to try it again." Or, if necessary, "Would you mind if we dropped the subject of the moment? I'm afraid I'm too touchy to discuss it further right now." (Keep in mind, however, that you had better come back to it later or the problem will continue to grow and rankle the two of you.)

In *Conjoint Family Therapy,* Virginia Satir echoes many of the above ideas and she says, "A person who communicates in a functional (healthy) way can (a) firmly state his case, (b) yet at the same time clarify and qualify what he says, (c) always ask for feedback, (d) and be receptive to feedback when he gets it." (5)

Some other ideas for dealing with an emotional situation in a healthy way are offered by Howard and Charlotte Clinebell in their book, *The Intimate Marriage:* "A couple may find it helpful to ask themselves questions such as these: Is this really an issue worth fighting over or is my self-esteem threatened by something my spouse has said or done? In relation to this issue or problem area, what do I want and what does my partner want that we are not getting? What must I give in the relationship in order to satisfy the needs of my partner, myself in this area? What small next step can we take right now toward implementing this decision, made jointly through the give-and-take of discussion?" (6)

WHAT DO YOU THINK? #20

"You are having a discussion with your mate. There are several noticeable differences of opinion. Soon voices and emotions begin to rise. You are starting to have some strong feelings toward what is going on and toward the other person. What should you do at this point?"

Describe how to deal with the above situation in an *unhealthy* manner:

Now write a dialogue of two people dealing with the situation in a healthy manner:

He:

She:

He:

She:

Practical Principles for Handling Anger

It helps to know what anger is, causes for anger, different kinds of responses to anger, what the Bible says about getting angry, healthy and unhealthy reactions to anger, etc., etc. But what finally counts is what you *do* with angry feelings when *you* have them. As a summary to this section on anger, here are ten practical principles for facing angry feelings and controlling them. Keep in mind, of course, that the Christian realizes he does not control anger (or any other problem) entirely in his own strength. He relies on the Holy Spirit to guide and empower. And never is the Holy Spirit needed more than when a person feels himself getting good and angry.

According to *The Living Bible* paraphrase of Galatians 5:19,20, when we follow our own wrong inclinations (the flesh) our lives produce evil results. And listed in those "evil results" are hatred and fighting, jealousy and anger . . . complaints and criticisms, the feeling that everyone else is wrong except you.

On the other hand, . . . *when the Holy Spirit controls our lives he will produce this kind of fruit in us: love, joy, peace, patience, kindness, goodness, faithfulness, gentleness and self-control* . . . (Gal. 5:22, *TLB*).

With the background, then, of the apostle Paul's words to the Galatians concerning how to handle anger and other basic emotions, here are ten practical steps you can take:

1. Be aware of your emotional reactions. Ask yourself, "What am I feeling?"

2. Recognize your emotions and admit that you have the feeling. Admitting the feeling of anger does not mean that you have to act it out.

3. Try to understand why you have anger. What brought it about? As mentioned in chapter 6, we are often angry because we are frustrated. We suffer from frustration of our desires, impulses, wants, ambitions, hopes, drives, hunger or will. When you are getting angry, ask yourself, "Does my anger come from frustration?" Then ask yourself, "What type of frustration?" Next, ask, "What or who is the cause of my frustration?" Ask yourself, "What positive solution can I think of?"

Other reasons why we get angry include:

The possibility of harm—physical harm or emotional harm. Our security is threatened and as a defense we become angry.

We become angry due to injustice—to others, ourselves or society. Often, this can be a "noble kind of anger" which is justified. But be careful and don't allow your righteous indignation over injustice become confused with another basic cause of anger which is: selfishness . . . the major cause of anger in most of us. If we are honest about it, we get mad because we aren't getting our own way. We aren't getting what we want.

4. Can you create other situations in which anger won't occur? What did you do to cause the other person to react in such a way that you became angry?

5. Is anger the best response? Write down the consequences of your getting angry. What is a better response? What would kindness, sympathy, understanding of the other person accomplish? Can you confess your feelings to him?

6. Is your anger the kind that rises too soon? If so, take some deep breaths or count to ten. Concentrate on the strengths and positive qualities of the other person instead of his defects.

7. Do you find yourself being critical of others? What does this do for you? Be less suspicious of other persons. Listen to what they say and feel. Evaluate their comments instead of condemning them. They may have something to offer to you. Does your criticalness or anger come from a desire to make yourself feel better? Are your opinions always accurate or could they be improved? Slow down in your speech and reactions toward others. Watch your gestures and expressions as they may convey rejection and criticism of the other person. Can you express appreciation and praise of the other in place of criticism?

8. You may have a time when your anger or criticism is legitimate. When you express it plan ahead and do it in such a way that the other person can accept what you say. Use timing, tact and have a desire to help the other person instead of tearing down.*

9. Find a friend with whom you can talk over your feelings and gain some insight from his suggestions. Admit how you feel and ask for his guidance.

10. Spend time praying for the difficulty that you have with your feelings. Openly admit your situation to God. Ask for His help. Memorize the Scriptures that speak of anger, and Scriptures that speak of how we should behave toward others. Memorize and understand them and put them into practice. (Review verses that talk about anger in chapter 6.)

How to Be Christian—and Angry

Yes, it is possible to be angry in a "Christian way." Christian anger, however, must fulfill three conditions:

It must be directed at something wrong and evil.

*An excellent book to read in this regard is David Augsburger's *Seventy Times Seven*, published by Moody, 1970.

CONFLICT CAN BE GOOD... IF

It must be controlled and not a heated, uncontrolled passion.

There must be no hatred, malice or resentment.

Three brief sentences—easily stated, not so easily lived—especially in marriage where feelings run deep and sensitivity is often at its highest pitch. But it can be done—even a tiny step at a time. It *must* be done if you and your mate are to learn how to handle anger and conflict.

In his excellent book, *After You've Said I Do,* Dwight Small points out, "As a reality in marriage, conflict can be creatively managed for good; it is part of the growth process. Don't ever underestimate its positive possibilities! . . . In Christian marriage conflict—with its demand for confession, forgiveness, and reconciliation—is a means God employs to teach humility." (7)

Ask yourself, "Do I really want to change and become more capable of handling anger, frustration and hostile feelings? Do I really want to creatively manage conflict for good?" If your answer is yes to these questions, then read Paul's prayer for the Ephesians (Eph. 3:16-21). Commit yourself anew to Christ and His love and take that love and the power of the Holy Spirit into your marriage—into the nitty-gritty arena where anger and frustration occur in various degrees almost daily. God's mighty power is at work within you and He is able to do far more than you would ever dare to ask or dream of—beyond your highest prayer, desires, thoughts or hopes!

WHAT'S YOUR PLAN?

If you are studying this book with your spouse, best results can be obtained if you complete the following material individually and then discuss your answers together. As you compare ideas, feelings and attitudes, you will achieve new levels of communication and understanding in your marriage relationship.

1. Describe the behavior or attitude that you want to change (for example: anger, anxiety, quarreling, yelling, etc.).

2. List several very personal reasons for giving up this behavior or attitude.

3. Motivation to change is very important. From your reasons for giving up the behavior or attitude, select the most important reason. Write it down.

4. Begin to think about how you should change your behavior if you wish to succeed. Write these down.

5. Adopt a positive attitude. What has been your attitude toward changing this in the past? Describe. Indicate what attitude you are going to have now. How will you maintain this new attitude? Write down your answer.

6. Whenever you eliminate a behavior or attitude that you dislike, often a vacuum or void will remain. Frequently a person prefers the bad or poor behavior to this emptiness so he reverts back to the previous pattern. In order for this not to happen, substitute a POSITIVE BEHAVIOR in place of the negative. Describe what you can substitute for the behavior or attitude that you are giving up.

7. Read Ephesians 4:31,32. List the positive behavior or attitude that this Scripture suggests in place of the negative. Write out the way you see yourself putting this Scripture into action in your life. Describe specific situations and describe how you picture yourself actually doing what the Scriptures suggest. Describe the consequences of thinking or behaving in this new way.

EXAMPLE

Ephesians 4:31,32

Negative Behavior or Attitude to STOP	List the results of this behavior. Give several for EACH one.
Bitterness (Resentfulness, harshness)	
Anger (Fury, antagonism, outburst)	
Wrath (Indignation, violent anger, boiling up)	
Clamor (Brawling)	
Slander (Abusive speech)	

Positive Behavior or Attitude to BEGIN	What do you think would be the results of doing these three commands? List several for each.
Kindness (goodness of heart)	
Tenderheartedness (compassionate)	
Forgiveness (an action)	

Now write out the practical ways in which you see yourself behaving or doing these things suggested in the verse.

List when and how you will begin and the consequences that you expect. Be very specific.

CHAPTER 8

the high cost of anxiety (and how not to pay it)

As you read this chapter, you will discover . . .

. . . that worry and anxiety are usually concerned with the past or the future, not the present

. . . that one spouse's anxiety or worry is almost sure to affect the other—and their marriage

. . . that Scripture contains practical advice for coping with anxiety and worry

. . . how to deal with pressures that cause worry and anxiety.

Anxiety and worry are common causes of trouble in marriage. When either marriage partner is tied in knots with fear and anxiety there is unhappiness. Hours spent in worry add up to discouraging, out-of-kilter days for both husband and wife, even if only one of them is the worrier.

Did you ever stop to think that worry has little to do with the present—except to make it miserable?

Worry is almost exclusively concerned with the past or the future. You dwell on past mistakes or what someone did to you yesterday . . . or what they didn't do or say. And before you know it you're having a terrible day all because you're concentrating on the past. True, it is often necessary to evaluate what happened and it is wise to learn from past experiences. But how much clearheaded evaluating and learning takes place when you worry? And, more important, did worry ever change yesterday?

Or maybe the past isn't what bothers you. It's the future that sends your worry out of control. You look at the bills and the financial obligations you will have to meet in the next six months and it's all too much to cope with. Perhaps you have a nagging health fear that you fret about, or possible future problems with your job. Whatever it is, when worry dominates your thinking you hardly have time to notice today.

No wonder marriages fall into deep trouble when worry consumes large chunks of energy of either the husband or the wife. Healthy, successful marriages need people committed to *today's* joys and problems. How much worry is there in your marriage? In your own life?

Did you ever analyze what you and your spouse worry about most often? Is it the past? What you could have said or should have done? Or is it the future that causes you to worry? Dreading what will happen to your children when they get out on their own? Concern about money for the bills that tie you in knots?

WHAT DO YOU THINK? #21

1. Think back over the last week. Did you spend the time feeling anxious or worried?

2. Were you aware of your mate being worried?

3. If worry was part of the past week, what specifically did you worry about? Do you know what your spouse worried about?

4. Can you list benefits or accomplishments that came as a result of your worry?

Defining Fear, Anxiety, Worry

God created man a thinking, emotional being. Because we are human we have the capacity to mull things over, to feel one way or another about a situation. Fear is one of the feelings all people experience from time to time. For example, fear that is based on external, real, physical dangers is healthy fear. It keeps us from being hurt by trucks, guns, hot stoves, etc.

Fear is an emotion and as such it becomes energy or a dynamic force. It is also an impulse to do something. When we refer to fear we think of such words as dismay, timidity, shyness, fright, alarm, panic, terror and horror. When we find that a person has fear we say that he is: afraid, alarmed, nervous, upset, disturbed, scared, fainthearted, shy, timid, bashful, diffident, frightened or aghast.

WORRYING DIVIDES YOUR MIND

What, then, is the difference between fear and anxiety? Anxiety is the feeling of apprehension, tension or uneasiness producing a sense of approaching danger, which does not stem from logic or a reasonable cause. Fear, on the other hand, is an emotional response that is consciously recognized, stimulated usually by some real threat (or at least it seems very real to the person who is afraid).

One way to see it is that fear is *external* and anxiety is *internal.* Anxiety can be defined as "fear in the absence of an adequate cause." Anxiety arises in response to danger and/or threat, yet often the source of this impending doom is not clear. The Greeks described anxiety as "opposing forces at work to tear a man apart."

We often use the word "worry" as a synonym for anxiety but this is not quite correct. The word "worry" means to fret, or be overly concerned. The person who worries spends great quantities of time thinking and dwelling upon a real or imagined problem. He goes over and over it in his mind. He usually begins thinking the worst about a situation and "crosses many bridges before he ever gets to them." The word "worry" comes from a combination of two words that mean "mind" and "divide." Worry means literally to "divide the mind."

The prophet Habakkuk gives a graphic description of a person involved in worry: *I heard and my inward parts trembled; at the sound my lips quivered. Decay enters my bones, and in my place I tremble. Because I must wait quietly for the day of distress* . . . (Hab. 3:16, *NASB*).

In his book *How to Win over Worry*, John Haggai comments that "Worry divides the feelings, therefore the emotions lack stability. Worry divides the understanding, therefore convictions are shallow and changeable. Worry divides the faculty of perception, therefore observations are faulty and even false. Worry divides the faculty of judging, therefore attitudes and decisions are often unjust. These decisions lead to damage and grief. Worry divides the determinative faculty, therefore plans, and purposes, if not 'scrapped' altogether, are not fulfilled with persistence." (1)

Worry and anxiety weaken and tear down a person. By contrast: *A calm and undisturbed mind and heart are the life and health of the body* . . . (Prov. 14:30, *Amplified).*

Are you consciously controlling worry in your life? Are you discovering ways to face your days with a "calm and undisturbed mind and heart"?

WHAT DO YOU THINK? #22

1. Can you pinpoint the one thing in your life that causes you the most anxiety and worry? If so, name it.

2. How would you describe this worry?

   Unhealthy   Healthy

3. Explain why you chose the description you did.

How You Can Win over Worry

Practically everyone agrees that anxiety and worry are destructive. But how does a person break out of worry patterns? The Bible gives the Christian practical guidelines for dealing with worry.

For example, Paul reminds the Christian . . . YOU ARE GOD'S CHILD. DEPEND ON YOUR HEAVENLY FATHER FOR HELP.

And now just as you trusted Christ to save you, trust him, too, for each day's problems; live in vital union with him. Let your roots grow down into him and draw up nourishment from him. See that you go on growing in the Lord, and become strong and vigorous in the truth you were taught. Let your lives overflow with joy and thanksgiving for all he has done (Col. 2:6,7, *TLB*).

Don't worry about anything, instead, pray about everything; tell God your needs and don't forget to thank him for his answers. If you do this you will. . . . keep your thoughts

HOW TO WIN OVER WORRY
PRESCRIPTION Nº 1

DEPEND ON GOD'S HELP

and your hearts quiet and at rest as you trust in Christ Jesus (Phil. 4:6,7, *TLB*).

When you read these instructions they sound so encouraging. Really great. But how do you put them to work to keep you from worrying? In essence Paul is saying:

Don't try to face your troubles on your own. Worry takes over when you look at a dark situation and you begin to fret, "This is awful. There's no way out. I'm sunk." That may (or may not) be true as far as you're concerned, but you're not alone. You can turn to God and tell Him how hard things are and trust Him for help. Depend on His power and strength to get you through.

Remember you have a choice of who "runs the ranch." Do your thoughts control you or do you control your thoughts? For example, when you wake up in the morning do worries take over and begin dictating your mood to you? Or do you say, "Hold it! Worry is not going to help." Get busy thinking about something else. Get busy doing something that demands your attention. Don't let worry "run your ranch." With God's help choose *not* to worry.

Concentrate on reality. Imagining what might happen or daydreaming about the consequences can lead to an extreme state of worry and anxiety. Face up to the actual situation and tell God your needs. As Paul says, *If you do this you will. . . . keep your thoughts and your hearts quiet and at rest as you trust in Christ Jesus.*

Be honest with yourself and accept your problems. Don't be afraid that you are "unspiritual" and "backslidden" because you are discouraged and worried. Don't worry about worrying; that will only make matters worse. Instead, honestly evaluate your feelings. Define your problem. And then follow Paul's advice: *. . . just as you trusted Christ to save you, trust him, too, for each day's problems.* It will help, too, if you thank God for the problem as well as His answer for it . . . even if you don't see a way out just at the moment. Remember what James wrote: *Is your life full of difficulties*

HOW TO WIN OVER WORRY
PRESCRIPTION NO. 2

FOCUS ON SOLUTIONS, NOT PROBLEMS

and temptations? Then be happy, for when the way is rough, your patience has a chance to grow. So let it grow, and don't try to squirm out of your problems (Jas. 1:2-4, *TLB*).

Jesus gave His disciples a sound principle for dealing with anxiety and fear . . . FOCUS ON THE SOLUTION RATHER THAN ON THE PROBLEM.

This principle is graphically illustrated in Matthew's account of Peter walking on the water: *And when the disciples saw Him walking on the sea, they were frightened, saying, "It is a ghost!" And they cried out for fear. But immediately Jesus spoke to them, saying, "Take courage, it is I; do not be afraid." And Peter answered Him and said, "Lord, if it is You, command me to come to You on the water." And He said, "Come!" And Peter got out of the boat, and walked on the water and came toward Jesus. But seeing the wind, he became afraid, and beginning to sink, he cried out, saying, "Lord, save me!" And immediately Jesus stretched out His hand and took hold of him, and said to him, "O you of little faith, why did you doubt?" And when they got into the boat, the wind stopped. And those who were in the boat worshiped Him, saying, "You are certainly God's Son!"* (Matt. 14:26-33, *NASB*).

Peter was fine as long as he stepped out on faith and kept his mind and his eyes on Christ. But when he focused his attention on the wind and the waves (his problems) they became overwhelming. Christ wants us to reach out in faith to Him and, depending on His help and guidance, to use the resources available to us and find workable solutions to our troubles. For example, try these "solution-oriented" ideas:

Think in terms of possible solutions. List your worries and anxieties. Be specific and complete in your descriptions. If you're really worried about the house payment this month don't just write "finances." Instead, put down "money for house payment" and any other pressing money problems you have. Then write a list of possible solutions. Your list

HOW TO WIN OVER WORRY
PRESCRIPTION No 3

TAKE ONE DAY AT A TIME.

may include borrowing, working an extra job, selling the antique clock, or even having a garage sale. Include every possibility you can think of and pray for God's help in choosing how you can move toward a solution.

Actively work on solutions. Thinking up possible solutions isn't enough. Act. For instance, if you feel that you worry far more than the average person and that something must be wrong with you, make an appointment with your doctor. Malfunction of glands, vitamin deficiencies, allergies, lack of exercise and emotional or physical fatigue can sometimes disguise themselves as worry or anxiety. As you look for reasons why you worry, rule out any possible physical causes to start with.

Don't concentrate on things that trouble you. When Peter concentrated on how high the waves were he began to sink. Recognize what increases your anxiety or worry. Stay away from those areas.

Suppose you and your spouse can't discuss politics without tensions building. Or maybe your mate follows the newscasts closely but you get upset and worried about the troubled world situation. Recognize the situation and work out a solution. When the news comes on maybe you should get busy in another part of the house with an activity you truly enjoy. Or help someone in the family who needs a hand.

One ex-worrier explains, "When I begin to get uptight and start to worry about how my husband and I have different views I get busy and thank God for all the blessings we've enjoyed together. Sometimes I even write out a list of blessings. When I start to 'name them one by one' somehow the worries don't seem important."

It helps to remember that Jesus taught His followers to . . . ACCEPT WHAT CAN'T BE CHANGED . . . KEEP KEY VALUES STRAIGHT . . . LIVE ONE DAY AT A TIME. See if you can pinpoint these principles in the following words on anxiety spoken by Christ: *For this reason I say to you, do not be anxious for your life, as to what you shall eat, or what you shall drink; nor for your body, as to what you shall put on. Is not life more than food, and the body than clothing? Look at the birds of the air, that they do not sow, neither do they reap, nor gather into barns; and yet your heavenly Father feeds them. Are you not worth much more than they? And which of you by being anxious can add a single cubit to his life's span? And why are you anxious about clothing? Observe how the lilies of the field grow; they do not toil nor do they spin, yet I say to you that even Solomon in all his glory did not clothe himself like one of these. But if God so arrays the grass of the field, which is alive today and tomorrow is thrown into the furnace, will He not much more do so for you, O men of little faith? Do not be anxious then, saying, "What shall we eat?" or, "What shall we drink?" or, "With what shall we clothe ourselves?" For all these things the Gentiles eagerly seek; for your heavenly Father knows that you need all these things. But seek first His kingdom, and His righteousness; and all these things shall be added to you. Therefore do not be anxious for tomorrow; for tomorrow will care for itself. Each day has enough trouble of its own* (Matt. 6:25-34, *NASB*).

Accepting what can't be changed, keeping key values straight, and living one day at a time can take much of the worry and anxiety out of a marriage relationship. Think through what would happen to trouble spots in your own marriage if you . . .

Accept what can't be changed. You've probably read Reinhold Niebuhr's prayer: "O God, give us serenity to accept what cannot be changed, courage to change what should be changed, and wisdom to distinguish the one from the other." What about making it a personal prayer that you really mean?

Face up to it that no amount of worry, nothing you can say, will really change your marriage partner. On the other hand, accepting your mate and loving him (or her) for what he (or she) is, can free each of you from worry. The changes in you may well be what God will use to help your marriage grow stronger and more satisfying.

In his book, *Are You Fun to Live With?*, Lionel Whiston tells of a man, Pete, who tried for years to change his wife to be more what he felt she should be. But "all he ever got in return was an argument or a brush-off."

Then Whiston goes on to say, "But a recent insight made a great difference to Peter . . . He has found greater joy in loving his family for what they are, not for what they might become.

"Pete still longs for the time when his wife will join him in Christian faith and often asks himself, 'When will my wife change and become a partner with me?' Then he answers, 'I don't know, and in a sense that is not my concern. My job is to love her, enjoy her, and be the finest husband and father that I can be. If God wants to change Arlene, he will. Meanwhile, I'm glad I married her.' " (2)

Keep values straight. What is worth worrying about? Are you worrying about the real issues? As *The Living Bible* puts Christ's words: *So my counsel is: Don't worry about things—food, drink, and clothes. For you already have life and a body—and they are far more important than what to eat and wear*" (Matt. 6:25).

As a Christian you enjoy God's forgiveness. You have the abundant life—life in God's family. Does remembering that help you take a clear look at your values?

Money may be tight; your clothes may be getting a little worn. You seem to be chalking up more failures than successes. As you work toward solutions for your problems, keep your values straight by remembering that "Christian security has little to do with success or failure. As Christians we believe that Christ loves us totally whether we succeed or fail." (3) He will help us with our needs as we rely on Him and His Word to help us get our values straight in every area of life.

Live one day at a time. Are you worrying about your

marriage, or enjoying it? Have you enjoyed your marriage partner today? Or are you too worried about what's coming up tomorrow to get the *now* into focus?

Of course the house needs a new roof and Johnny's teeth should be straightened, and you can't wait much longer to have the brakes on your car relined. Even so, Jesus says, "Don't be anxious about tomorrow. God will take care of your tomorrow too. Live one day at a time." Do you believe that? You'd better. Today's the only day you have.

WHAT DO YOU THINK? #23

1. Go back through the Biblical principles for dealing with worry. Choose one or two ideas that are especially meaningful to you.

2. Now think of ways you want to use the ideas to help you move from worry to a place of greater freedom and trust in God.

3. Can you think of at least one way trust and confidence in God—instead of worry—will be strengthening to your marriage? Be specific.

Stress Can Be Good for Your Marriage

A final word about problems and stress—the things that make you worry.

Stressful situations can be valuable situations as far as your marriage is concerned. As Dwight Small says, "Life's most trying moments can also be times of communicating at new depths of mutual understanding. It is the experience of couples who have been married for a long while that some of their best times of dialogue have come during setbacks. The loss of a job, sickness of a child, death of a parent—such experiences necessarily bring about a need for cooperation and decisive action. This makes two people sense their need of one another in special ways." (4)

When troubles come, instead of letting worry make you weak and miserable, reach out to God and reach out to your mate, confident that together you can face each day.

WHAT'S YOUR PLAN?

1. Read the following Scripture passage and write down *what* we are to do and *why* we are to do it: *Casting the whole of your care—all your anxieties, all your worries, all*

your concerns, once and for all—on Him; for He cares for you affectionately, and cares about you watchfully (1 Pet. 5:7, *Amplified*).

What I am to do:

Why I am to do it:

2. What is the plan for the elimination of anxiety or worry in the following passage? *You will guard him and keep him in perfect and constant peace whose mind [both its inclination and its character] is stayed on You, because he commits himself to You, leans on You and hopes confidently in You* (Isa. 26:3, *Amplified*).

The word "mind" refers to our imagination or thought life. What do you think or dwell upon?

3. Read the following Scripture passage: *Do not fret or have any anxiety about anything, but in every circumstance and in everything by prayer and petition, [definite requests] with thanksgiving continue to make your wants known to God. And God's peace [be yours, that tranquil state of a soul assured of its salvation through Christ, and so fearing nothing from God and content with its earthly lot of whatever sort that is, that peace] which transcends all understanding, shall garrison and mount guard over your hearts and minds in Christ Jesus.*

For the rest, brethren, whatever is true, whatever is worthy of reverence and is honorable and seemly, whatever is just, whatever is pure, whatever is lovely and lovable, whatever is kind and winsome and gracious, if there is any virtue and excellence, if there is anything worthy of praise, think on and weigh and take account of these things—fix your minds on them (Phil. 4:6-8, *Amplified*).

List your anxieties:

List your definite requests:

List some specific things to think of that meet the qualifications of verse 8:

The next time you start to worry, think of Philippians 4:8 and concentrate on what is worthy of reverence, honorable, just, pure, lovely, kind, winsome, gracious. Get together with your spouse and isolate a particular anxiety or worry that each of you has. Make these a matter of prayer and use the verses you have studied above for inspiration to literally forget your troubles and anxieties.

CHAPTER 9

how to cope with conflict

As you read this chapter, you will discover . . .
. . . that conflict is part of marriage and should be handled, not hidden or ignored
. . . some major causes for conflict and what to do about them
. . . ten key principles (with several valuable sub-principles) for coping successfully with conflict, according to the teaching of Scripture.

Sugar-coated myths picture marriage as the time when you "live happily ever after" (particularly if you are Christians!). Fighting and disagreeing, say the myths, are just not part of a healthy, "spiritual" marriage.

But the sugar coating quickly melts away under the heat of married reality. Marriage *does* include conflict, because a marriage is a union of two individuals who have unique viewpoints, frames of reference, and values. No two people can agree on everything all the time. In any marriage there will be conflict from time to time.

What exactly is conflict? For some the word conjures up scenes of battlegrounds and warfare. This is one of the meanings of conflict, but the meaning with which this chapter is concerned is, according to Webster, "Disagreement, emotional tension resulting from incompatible inner needs or drives."

That definition is a challenge for every married couple. How can they handle their disagreements—the tensions that come when the needs and drives of one spouse are at cross-purposes with the other? How do they keep cross-purposes from becoming crossed swords?

Every married couple needs to know how to deal with conflict in a creative, constructive way.

Objectivity, flexibility, willingness to compromise (Is squeezing the toothpaste tube at the bottom rather than in the middle *really* one of the big issues of life?) and the willingness to let the other person be himself, all need to be developed if couples are to enjoy a satisfying and growing marriage relationship.

When conflict comes, it should be faced with the understanding that disagreements do not mean that the entire relationship is on the verge of breaking down. Nor should a disagreement be a trigger for a knock-down, drag-out scrap (verbal and/or physical). Husbands and wives need to know how to "disagree agreeably" or to put it in a little stronger terms, "fight fair." Unfortunately, few couples get any training on how to "disagree agreeably" and "fight fair" before marriage. As a result, their disagreements often turn into spats, heated arguments and quarrels. All of this really isn't necessary. Any couple can cope better with conflict if they use the following ten principles.

Don't Avoid Conflict with the Silent Treatment

Some people use the "silent treatment" as a means of avoiding controversy. They use silence as a weapon to control, frustrate or manipulate their spouse. Or sometimes the husband or wife takes the pathway of silence because it seems to be the least painful. Perhaps one spouse is silent now because in the past the other spouse was not a ready listener. Also, there's always the possibility of a deep hurt that is keeping one marriage partner silent.

But silence never pays off in the long run. "Silence is golden" so the saying goes, but it can also be yellow! Don't hide behind silence because you are afraid to deal with the issue at hand.

Marriage counselors estimate that at least one half of the cases they see involve a silent husband. Men have a tendency to avoid conflict in discussion. Ironically, the issues they avoid are often the ones that indicate where adjustments and changes need to be made—and fast.

Here is a typical pattern that results in the use of silence. When married partners are not communicating because one of them is silent, both of them experience frustration and a rising sense of futility, all of which compounds the silence problem. The more the communicative person tries to talk, the farther the silent person draws into his hostile shell. The person who is trying to talk then feels increasingly useless, inadequate and hurt. The talkative spouse may try shouting, or even violence, in an attempt to drive the silent mate from his refuge. But this is futile because it does nothing more than to drive the silent spouse into deeper silence. When you say to a silent person, "Why don't you talk to me?" or

"Please say something—why can't we communicate?" or similar pleas, it usually does nothing more than reinforce that person's silence! (1)

How, then, do you encourage the silent person to talk? First, you have to let the silent partner choose the time to speak. Then, when this person does speak, you must communicate in every way you can that you're willing to listen without judging what is said; that you are willing to accept feelings and frustrations. The silent person must find that you really do listen and care. If you create an acceptant, unthreatening climate, the silent spouse will in all likelihood start talking and then communication can begin or be reestablished.

WHAT DO YOU THINK? #24

1. Circle how you *tend* to respond when controversy arises:

talk incessantly   clam up

2. List several reasons you think a person might choose to be silent:

3. When would it be best for you to be silent?

Why?

Will your silence solve the problem or improve communication in the long run?

4. Write down several things you can do to encourage a silent mate to be more expressive.

Don't Save "Emotional Trading Stamps"

Always watch yourself to make sure you're not saving up hostility yourself. A husband or wife, for example, could easily save up a lot of hostility when trying to deal with a mate who is dealing out the silent treatment (discussed above). But the worst method of dealing with feelings of irritation or frustration is to deny them and bottle them up. Feelings must be expressed. They shouldn't be allowed to accumulate.

Some individuals, however, deal with their emotions like trading stamps. They save up each little irritation as though

EMOTIONAL TRADING STAMPS AREN'T WORTH SAVING

it were a stamp. They accumulate many stamps and, finally, when something happens that is the last straw, they blow up and "cash in" with all of their pent-up irritations and frustrations. Their emotional trading-stamp book becomes full, and they decide that now is the time to trade it in. In this way they think "they get something back" for all of their trouble. They "redeem their trading stamps," so to speak, and tell themselves, "Well, now at least I feel better."

Are you an emotional stamp saver? If you suspect that you are, now is the time to start doing something about it. It is much better to release your emotions as they *arise*. God created all of us to feel deeply, but we must express what we feel. Our expressions should, and can be done, in a healthy way.

Much of the arguing, quarreling, fighting that occurs between married couples turns into sadistic, emotionally crippling sessions. How do *you* handle your disagreements?

A crucial question is how you handle anger—those strong, even passionate feelings of displeasure that well up within? How does your anger handle you? (At this point you may want to review Chapters 6 and 7 on handling anger.)

Suppose your spouse acts negatively toward you or even gets angry with you. Ask yourself these questions:

Am I really being hurt or affected by this?

Will counter-anger, even if it's justified and rational, really help here?

Is getting angry the most effective thing I can do?

What will my anger accomplish?

How do I respond to or answer another person who is angry? Whatever you do, do not tell the other person, "Now don't get angry." When you say this, it has exactly the opposite effect! Instead, try saying as quietly as you can, "I'm sorry something is making you angry. If it's me, I apologize. What can I do to help?" This suggestion is effective at home, at work—just about anywhere. Strangely enough it sounds vaguely familiar—"like something from the Bible." Solomon, who had quite a bit of marital experience, once wrote, *A soft answer turns away wrath* (Prov. 15:1, *Amplified*).

WHAT DO YOU THINK? #25

1. List several ways you can express anger without hurting yourself or others.

2. State the way in which you wish your mate would let you know he or she is angry.

3. How can you let your spouse know that you would prefer that his or her anger be communicated differently?

If Possible, Prepare the Setting for Disagreement

If you have a major discussion on an important topic coming up, try to arrange for the best time and place. Guard against interruption. You may want to take the phone off the hook, or not answer the door. If you have children, ask them not to interrupt you. If the children do interrupt you, let them know that you are having an important discussion and you will talk to them when you are finished.

Parents do not usually succeed in hiding disagreements and arguments from their children. Let them know that you do disagree sometimes and that all family members will have times of disagreement. Keep in mind that your children will learn their pattern for disagreeing and arguing from watching you. If you can establish healthy patterns for disagreement with your spouse, it can do a lot to help your children learn to disagree in a healthy way—all of which can add to peace and harmony around the house.

Attack the Problem, Not Each Other

Do your best to keep the discussion impersonal. Instead of attacking the problem, too many couples attack each other with innuendos, slurs and other "smart" remarks.

There is an old story about a sheepherder in Wyoming who would observe the behavior of wild animals during the winter. Packs of wolves, for example, would sweep into the valley and attack the bands of wild horses. The horses would form a circle with their heads at the center of the circle and kick out at the wolves, driving them away. Then the sheepherder saw the wolves attack a band of wild jackasses. The animals also formed a circle, but they formed it with their heads out toward the wolves. When they began to kick, they ended up kicking one another.

People have a choice between being as smart as a wild horse or as stupid as a wild jackass. They can kick the problem or they can kick one another. Here are five tips to help

SHORT COURSE IN ATTACKING EACH OTHER INSTEAD OF THE PROBLEM

you kick the problem—to disagree without kicking your spouse:

. . . back up any accusation or statement that you make with facts.

. . . stay in the present. Complaints over six months old are not permissible. Avoid saying, "I remember when. . . ." There is a sign over one businessman's desk that reads, "Remember to Forget." Every couple needs to place that very sign over their marriage. The apostle Paul said, . . . *I am bringing all my energies to bear on this one thing: Forgetting the past and looking forward to what lies ahead . . .* (Phil. 3:13, *TLB*).

. . . Do not make references to relatives or in-laws.

. . . Do not make references to your mate's appearance. That is, refrain from injecting jabs and cutting remarks about overweight, falling hair, sloppy clothes, etc.

. . . No dramatics, please. No getting highly emotional and exploding into tears. Crying is often a means of manipulating the other person. Threats are also used for manipulation. Some spouses even threaten suicide as an attempt to control their mates. But none of these methods usually help. There are no Oscars for dramatics when married people are trying to work out a disagreement.

WHAT DO YOU THINK? #26

What if your spouse attacks you instead of the problem?

1. If an accusation or statement is made which is not backed up with facts, I will say:

2. When a complaint that is over six months old is raised, I will state:

3. If a reference is made to an in-law or relative, I will:

4. If I make a reference to my mate's appearance, I will:

5. If a reference is made to my appearance, I will:

6. When either I or my mate becomes "dramatic," I will:

7. Review your answers to the above six situations. Are your answers positive or negative? Will they help or hurt your mate? Will they make communication more effective next time or will they tend to hinder future communication? If your answers are negative, hurtful, or will tend to hinder future communication, rewrite them!

Don't "Throw Your Feelings" at Your Spouse

Learn how to inform your spouse of your feelings. Don't hurl them like a spear or a rock.

Dr. Howard Clinebell suggests that a ". . . road to productive communication is for both husband and wife to learn the skill of *saying it straight*. Each person can help the other to understand by asking himself, 'Am I saying what I really mean?' This involves learning to be aware of what one is actually feeling and developing the ability to put the feeling clearly into words. Direct rather than devious, specific rather than generalized statements are required. A wife criticizes her husband as he sits at the breakfast table hidden behind his newspaper, 'I wish you wouldn't always slurp your coffee.' What she really means is, 'I feel hurt when you hide in the newspaper instead of talking to me.' Saying it straight involves being honest about negative as well as positive feelings, and being able to state them in a non-attacking way: 'I feel . . . ,' rather than 'You are. . . .' Some risk is required in the beginning of this kind of communication, until both husband and wife can trust the relationship enough to be able to say what they really mean.

"James Farmer tells a story about a woman who acquired wealth and decided to have a book written about her genealogy. The well-known author she engaged for the assignment discovered that one of her grandfathers had been electrocuted in Sing Sing. When he said it would have to be included in the book, she pleaded for a way of saying it that would hide the truth. When the book appeared, it read as follows: 'One of her grandfathers occupied the chair of applied electricity in one of America's best known institutions. He was very much attached to his position and literally died in the harness.' The meaning in some attempts to communicate between marriage partners is almost as hidden and confusing. It is usually better to 'say it like it is,' gently if necessary, but clearly." (2)

In the words of the Preacher: *There is a right time for everything: . . . a time to be quiet; a time to speak up* (Eccl. 3:1,7, *TLB*).

Stay on the Subject

Always try to discover exactly what you are arguing about and stay on that subject. Don't bring in matters that are irrelevant or unimportant. At times you may have to say something like, "Let's stop this conversation and really see what it is we're talking about. You start again and I will listen. Perhaps I have misunderstood something." Take the initiative to do this yourself. Don't wait for your spouse to do so. Always be willing to listen and ask questions.

As you are engaging in an argument or an important discussion, remember to ask yourself, "Is there really as much of a problem or difference of opinion here as I think? Am I seeking a real solution or just looking for problems?" Do you tend to see the dark or the bright side of things? Do you spend a lot of time going over and over problems in your mind? Do you literally create problems in your own mind?

The answer to these questions may lie in whether you are an optimist or a pessimist. The difference is easy to see in this old but still humorous story:

"There were two farmers. One was a pessimist, the other was an optimist.

"The optimist would say, 'Wonderful sunshine.'

"The pessimist would respond, 'Yeah, I'm afraid it's going to scorch the crops.'

"The optimist would say, 'Fine rain.'

"The pessimist would respond, 'Yeah, I'm afraid we are going to have a flood.'

"One day the optimist said to the pessimist. 'Have you seen my new bird dog? He's the finest money can buy.'

"The pessimist said, 'You mean that mutt I saw penned up behind your house? He don't look like much to me.'

"The optimist said, 'How about going hunting with me tomorrow?' The pessimist agreed. They went. They shot some ducks. The ducks landed on the pond. The optimist ordered his dog to get the ducks. The dog obediently responded. Instead of swimming in the water after the ducks, the dog walked on top of the water, retrieved the ducks, and walked back on top of the water.

"The optimist turned to the pessimist and said, 'Now, what do you think of that?'

"Whereupon the pessimist replied, 'Hmmm, he can't swim, can he?' "(3)

Aren't we all like that at times? We can't see the good or the strong points of our spouse because we focus on faults or problems. Perhaps it wouldn't hurt for every husband and wife to memorize Philippians 4:8,9:

Fix your thoughts on what is true and good and right. Think about things that are pure and lovely, and dwell on the fine, good things in others. Think about all you can praise God for and be glad about. Keep putting into prac-

tice all you learned from me and saw me doing, and the God of peace will be with you (*TLB*).

Offer Solutions with Criticisms

If you criticize your spouse, can you offer a clear-cut solution at the same time? To say, "The way you leave your dirty clothes lying around makes our bedroom look like a pigpen" really doesn't help. Saying, "Would it help keep our bedroom neater if I moved the clothes hamper into the bedroom so we wouldn't have to walk so far?" offers a solution to the problem and also communicates displeasure with the status quo.

Another good verse of Scripture for husbands and wives to remember and apply is:

Let us therefore stop turning critical eyes on one another. If we must be critical, let us be critical of our own conduct and see that we do nothing to make a brother stumble or fall (Rom. 14:13, *Phillips*).

Never "analyze" your spouse during a discussion. Don't play physician or psychiatrist by saying things like, "Now you are saying that because. . . ." Your spouse is not a case study. He or she is part of you—one flesh—your mate!

Never Say, "You Never" or "You Always"

There's nothing like the sweeping statement or the vast generalization to increase the difficulty. Avoid words like "never," "always," "all," "everyone."

Avoid loaded statements such as:

"You're never on time."

"You're always saying things like that."

"All women are emotional."

"All men are like that."

"Everyone thinks you are that way, and so do I!"

Two other excellent ways to decrease difficulty in a conversation are these:

Watch your volume.

Don't exaggerate.

Most of us tend to raise our voices during family discussions. When we do this, we are really saying, "I can't get through to you in a normal voice because you seem to be deaf to what I say. So I will turn up the volume."

Raising our voice puts our spouse on the defense and can even convey that we have lost control—of our temper, or the situation.

It's easy to add to your problems by exaggerating. We seem to think that the facts as they are do not make any impression upon our spouse, so we try to get our spouse's attention by altering the facts or "dressing them up a little bit."

The sweeping generalization is a typical way that we exaggerate.

She says, "You never finish anything you start around here. You've been working on that fence for the last six months!"

He says, "You're always late. You make us late when we go out to dinner, to the theatre, to P.T.A., to church. We're going to be late for our funeral!"

A verse from Ephesians contains good advice for spouses who exaggerate:

. . . lovingly follow the truth at all times—speaking truly, dealing truly, living truly—and so become more and more in every way like Christ . . . (Eph. 4:15, *TLB*).

Don't Use Criticism to Become a Comedian

While it's true that a joke or dry remark might relieve the tension in some marital disagreements, it's always best to use humor with care. Never try to be funny by criticizing your spouse. The problem might not be serious to you, but it might be very important to your mate.

Questions to ask before using humor are:

"Will this increase tension or relieve it?"

"Can I laugh at myself, or am I just trying to poke fun at my mate?"

"Am I trying to win points for my side with cute remarks?"

When You're Wrong, Admit It; When You're Right, Shut Up

Have the humility to remember that you could be wrong. A lot of people find this sentence difficult if not impossible to say: "I'm wrong—you may be right." Practice saying it by yourself if necessary and then be able to say it when it fits into a disagreement or discussion. When you honestly own up to knowing that you're wrong and the other person is right, you improve communication a thousandfold and deepen your relationship with your spouse.

And when it is appropriate, always ask for forgiveness. James tells us to admit our faults to one another and pray for each other. (See James 5:16 in *The Living Bible.)*

Proverbs 28:13 has good advice: *A man who refuses to admit his mistakes can never be successful. But if he confesses and forsakes them, he gets another chance* (*TLB*).

Sometimes you will have to admit you're wrong in the face of your spouse's criticism, and this is never easy. It can also be tricky. Be sure that you never play the "I know it's all *my* fault" game with your mate. It is easy to use the line "It's all *my* fault" as a means of manipulating your mate. The idea is that you get your mate feeling apologetic and saying, "Well, I suppose it's partially my fault too. . . ."

If you are really at fault, then be willing to admit it. Saying something like, "You know, I do think that I am to blame here. I'm sorry that I said that and that I hurt you. What can I do now to help or make up for this?"

When you face your spouse's criticism and you know it's correct, keep these proverbs in mind:

If you refuse criticism you will end in poverty and disgrace; if you accept criticism you are on the road to fame (Prov. 13:18, *TLB*).

Don't refuse to accept criticism; get all the help you can (Prov. 23:12, *TLB*).

It is a badge of honor to accept valid criticism (Prov. 25:12, *TLB*).

And when your spouse confesses faults or admits error, be sure to tell him or her of your forgiveness. Even if you were right, take the initiative to forgive *and forget.* Proverbs 17:9 teaches, *Love forgets mistakes* (*TLB*). Colossians 3:13 says that we should *be gentle and ready to forgive; never hold grudges (TLB).*

In summary, the apostle Peter and Ogden Nash have words of good advice.

Peter tells us, *Most important of all, continue to show*

"To keep
your marriage brimming
with love
in the loving cup
When you're wrong
admit it,
when you're right,
shut up."

Ogden Nash

deep love for each other, for love makes up for many of your faults (1 Pet. 4:8, *TLB*).

Ogden Nash once gave this word to husbands (which also is certainly appropriate for wives):

"To keep your marriage brimming with love in the loving cup,
When you're wrong admit it,
When you're right shut up."

WHAT'S YOUR PLAN?

1. Reprinted below are the "Ten Principles for Coping with Conflict." Review them and check off the ones where you feel fairly strong and capable. Go over them again and underline the ones where you feel weak—"in need of more practice."

Ten Ways to Cope with Conflict

1. Don't avoid conflict with the silent treatment.
2. Don't save "emotional trading stamps."
3. If possible, prepare the setting for disagreement.
4. Attack the problem, not each other . . .
   . . . back up accusations with facts
   . . . remember to forget
   . . . no cracks about in-laws or relatives
   . . . no cracks about your mate's appearance
   . . . no dramatics.
5. Don't throw your feelings like stones.
6. Stay on the subject.
7. Offer solutions with your criticisms.
8. Never say, "You never . . ."
   . . . turn down the volume
   . . . don't exaggerate.
9. Don't manipulate your mate with, "It's all *my* fault."
10. Be humble—you could be wrong.

2. Are you an optimist or a pessimist? How does your mate experience you? (circle one).

"Oh, boy!" "Oh, no!"

Read and memorize Philippians 4:8,9.

3. List at least three specific changes in behavior you will make, which are based on the "Ten Principles for Coping with Conflict."

4. Get together with your mate and share your findings from doing the above exercises. (A word of caution: apply the principles to *yourself*. Don't infer that "A lot of these are really *your* mate's problem," or you may wind up in a disagreement (conflict) over this chapter on coping with conflict. If you do get into a disagreement, be sure to use the Ten Principles and "fight fair!" Good luck!

CHAPTER 10

communicate to build self-esteem

As you read this chapter, you will discover . . .
. . . that building your mate's self-esteem is one of your most important goals in marriage communication
. . . that it's more important to seek to understand your mate than to worry about your mate understanding you
. . . that there are ten practical principles for building self-esteem in your marriage partner
. . . how to plan to use the ten principles for building self-esteem to improve communication in your marriage.

If you have stuck with this book to this point, you have . . .

. . . discovered that you are already a fairly good communicator and have probably picked up some tips to help you be even better.

. . . or improved on your communication skills in several ways.

. . . or, at least have taken some small steps toward communicating at deeper levels with your spouse.

No matter where you are as husband and wife, you will want to keep communication lines open. A key to communication—perhaps *the* key—is building your mate's self-esteem. A person's self-esteem is his overall judgment of himself—how much he likes his particular person. High self-esteem doesn't mean you are on a continual ego-trip. High self-esteem means you have solid feelings of self-respect and self-worth. You are glad you are you. (1)

Marriage partners with high self-esteem are bound to be happier and communicate better. High self-esteem means an absence or at least a considerable lessening of anxieties, complexes, hangups, and the other problems that prevent good communications. The spouse with low self-esteem is seldom a good communicator. Low self-esteem often drives a person into a shell of silence or compels a person to become a dominating over-talkative, unacceptant dictator in one-way communication—"*my way.*"

This final chapter is dedicated to the continuing challenge of building your mate's self-esteem—making him or her feel important, wanted, valuable, successful and, above all, loved. Following are ten practical principles for building self-esteem in your mate.

Make It Safe to Communicate

Strive to establish and maintain a permissive atmosphere in your home. In a permissive atmosphere both marriage partners are free to share openly and honestly what they

feel, think and believe. Each family member is allowed to speak the truth in love. The husband, or the wife, does not consciously erect barriers to communication with his or her mate.

Sometimes a spouse tells his mate, "I didn't tell you that because I was afraid of hurting you." In giving this kind of an excuse, a spouse is sometimes hiding behind a pretense of being concerned about his mate's feelings. This kind of cop-out seldom does anything to build the kind of open communication that is needed in a marriage. Perhaps speaking the truth will hurt, perhaps it will not. Too often, marriage partners avoid constructive discussions because they feel that they would have to make changes in their own lives if any communication would take place on that kind of level.

Dr. John Drakeford gives the following guidelines for an open permissive communication in the home:

"1. Look at the positive aspects of openness. When a man

and his wife live in such a close relationship they should not have large areas of experience which they hide from each other.

"2. Surely there must come a time when we sit down and say to our mate: 'Honey, you have a right to know who you married. Let me tell you about myself.'

"3. One of the most reprehensible uses of openness is to use it as a means of attack. 'Yes, this is what I did but the reason I did it was that you were so cold to me,' is not honesty, it is attack.

"4. Let us be honest about ourselves without excuse or justification. When we have made a mistake, admit it.

"5. Two parties must play their parts in the process—no one should ever sit in judgment on anybody else." (2)

Dr. Drakeford's five rules are worth following and they parallel closely the principles for coping with conflict given in Chapter 9. But what about times when it seems that openness and honesty may do more harm than good? Aren't there times in a marriage when it is more loving to lie (just a little, perhaps?) than to speak the truth? Isn't it better to lie on certain occasions if it means that you can avoid unpleasantness in your marriage relationship—if you can avoid hurting your spouse?

We can all think of situations in which it would probably be best not to speak the truth because it will hurt our marriage partner. But does lying really avoid unpleasantness in the long run? Lies—even gentle white lies told to keep the peace—have a way of being discovered and when they are discovered there is even more unpleasantness.

When you consider lying to avoid unpleasantness you should be brutally honest with your motivation. Are you really afraid of hurting your spouse? Or is it yourself that you're worried about? Are you just trying to ease out of an unpleasant situation because it isn't worth the hassle?

Often temptations to lie come when we are confronted

with something that we have done. We are tempted to alter the truth or rationalize the facts in order to deflect the blame away from ourselves. This pattern starts when we are small children. When small children are confronted with wrong behavior they find it difficult, if not impossible, to say, "Yes, I did it. I'm sorry."

Have you ever noticed the reaction of other people when you accept responsibility for your actions and are open and truthful about them? To tell the truth, to admit errorr or wrongdoing, to "let the buck stop with you," often brings reactions from others of amazement if not downright shock!

There may be times when to hold back part of the truth seems to be the best thing to do because the other person may not be ready for all the facts at a certain point in time. But keep in mind when you do this—when you hold back part of the information—you are causing your spouse to think the opposite of what the truth really is. When you do this, you gamble—with your spouse's feelings and certainly with keeping communication lines in good repair. Think it through carefully. Is the gamble really worth it?

Seek to Understand, Not to Be Understood

Spend as much time and effort trying to understand your mate's viewpoint as you do trying to make him or her understand yours. Perhaps there's a good and legitimate reason for your spouse's beliefs, actions or habits. Everyone's background and environment are different and they bring this background with them to the marriage relationship.

When one spouse sulks, stews or balks because the other "doesn't understand," what is really being said? The real message is, "You don't understand *me*! You don't want to adjust to my ideas and way of doing things. You don't want to give me my way!"

If both spouses start saying, "You don't understand," then there is an even more serious problem—and very little communication. There is, however, a way out of the problem of

being "misunderstood." Paul Tournier pinpoints the solution as he says:

"You well know that beautiful prayer of Francis of Assisi: 'Lord! Grant that I may seek more to understand than to be understood. . . .' It is this new desire which the Holy Spirit awakens in couples and which transforms their marriage. As long as a man is preoccupied primarily with being understood by his wife, he is miserable, overcome with self-pity, the spirit of demanding, and bitter withdrawal. As soon as he becomes preoccupied with understanding her, seeking to understand that which he had not before understood, and with his own wrongdoing in not having understood her, then the direction taken by events begins to change. As soon as a person feels understood, he opens up and because he lowers his defenses he is also able to make himself better understood." (3)

Tournier feels so strongly about the need for understanding one another that he says the husband and wife should become *preoccupied* with it—lost in it—engrossed to the fullest in learning what makes the other one tick, what the other one likes, dislikes, fears, worries about, dreams of, believes in and *why* he or she feels this way.

As is so often the case, Scripture has taught this kind of basic truth for centuries. Long ago the apostle Paul directed the Ephesians to live in a becoming way, . . . *with complete lowliness of mind (humility) and meekness (unselfishness, gentleness, mildness), with patience, bearing with one another and making allowances because you love one another* (Eph. 4:2, *Amplified*).

And Paul had the same thing in mind when he wrote the Philippians and said,

Fill up and complete my joy by living in harmony and being of the same mind and one in purpose, having the same love, being in full accord and of one harmonious mind and intention. Do nothing from factional motives—through contentiousness, strife, selfishness or for unworthy ends—or prompted by conceit and empty arrogance. Instead, in the true spirit of humility (lowliness of mind) let each regard the others as better than and superior to himself—thinking more highly of one another than you do of yourselves. Let each of you esteem and look upon and be concerned for not [merely] his own interests, but also each for the interests of others (Phil. 2:2-4, *Amplified*).

The cry, "You don't understand!" is the childish whine of an immature mate who is playing games with his or her marriage partner. The prayer of St. Francis, "Lord! Grant that I may seek more to understand than to be understood . . ." is the honest plea of the husband or wife who wants to communicate—who wants to build a sound and successful marriage by building up the other partner.

WHAT DO YOU THINK? #27

1. State what ". . . making allowances because you love one another" means to you in regard to your spouse:

2. State what looking upon and being concerned ". . . for the interests of others" means to you in regard to your spouse:

Don't Assume You Know—Ask

Recognize that there is some information you cannot get

by any other means than by asking your spouse about it. Never assume that you know what your spouse thinks. Have you ever heard a husband saying, "My wife thinks . . ."? How does he really know? Does he *really* know she thinks or believes that? Or is he just taking it for granted? Has he asked her? Has he ever really discussed the matter?

Assumption about what your spouse knows, thinks or feels is dangerous. True, it is easy to get impressions about what people believe from the non-verbal language they use —their looks, glances and mannerisms. But if you really want to know what your spouse is thinking, start talking about it. Husband-wife communication will automatically improve if both stop assuming and start communicating. Some night soon (or right now) turn off the tube and talk together about the following ideas.

WHAT DO YOU THINK? #28

1. Write down what you think your mate believes about each of these subjects:

The role of the husband

The role of the father

The role of the wife

The role of the mother

Male and female tasks in the home

Politics

Women's lib

Sex

The importance of a creative outlet for the husband

The importance of a creative outlet for the wife

Recreation together as a couple/family

2. Now compare notes and discuss what you assumed and what is actual fact.

Listen—Don't Interrupt

Much has been said in earlier chapters (4 and 5) about listening, but enough can't be said about this skill, which is so rusty with disuse (or practically nonexistent) in so many marriages.

It may well be true that the first duty of love is to listen. Dr. S. S. Hayakawa says, "We can, if we are able to listen as well as to speak, become better informed and wiser as we grow older, instead of being stuck like some people with the same little bundle of prejudices at sixty-five that we had at twenty-five."

But listening takes discipline. We fail to listen to our spouse because of impatience and a lack of concentration, especially when he or she is saying something that we don't particularly want to hear.

Perhaps it is hardest to listen when your spouse picks a poor time to bring something up. For example, you come

I WANT TO TALK TO YOU ABOUT SOMETHING.
AT ONE O'CLOCK IN THE MORNING?

home late at night, exhausted, and your spouse is already in bed, asleep (or so you think). You get ready for bed, wearily crawl in and are just ready for dreamland, when all of a sudden you find out your spouse wasn't sleeping at all. She's been waiting for you and she says, "I'd like to talk to you about something that's been bothering me quite a bit."

Your initial reaction might well be, "Of all the dumb times to bring up something. Why doesn't she do it during the day and not at this ridiculous hour? Can't she see that it's late and I'm beat?"

Granted this kind of timing is hardly the best but before you plead to "let's talk about it tomorrow," think it through. Why has she waited so long to bring something up? Why wait until you're both in bed and it's easy to hide in the darkness? Could there be something you might have done to make it difficult for your partner to talk about what is on her mind? Consider these questions before you react. You might learn something if you pause to listen, too!

There are other common problems concerning not listening and interrupting. For example, there is the "keep the record straight" type. The typical dialogue goes something like this. The husband is talking, starting to tell some mutual friends a story . . .

"We left about the middle of July."

"Oh, no dear, it was actually the twenty-seventh."

"OK, so we left the twenty-seventh about nine o'clock in the morning . . ."

"Oh, I'm sorry, dear, but it was seven-thirty exactly. I remember looking at the clock as I checked the doors."

"Well, we left sometime and drove to San Francisco."

"Are you sure we drove there that first day? Wasn't it . . .?"

It's easy to get the picture here! The wife is "over-listening" but not because she wants to hear what her husband is saying. She wants to keep the record straight!

And then there is the "outguesser" type. This person

usually is one step ahead of you and unfortunately he really believes that he is listening. But he never lets you finish what you were going to say. Wives have a tendency to try to outguess their husbands, as in the following example:

"Honey, I was at the store today . . ."

"Don't tell me you forgot the list?"

"No, I wasn't going to say that. I said I went to the store today and I saw John . . ."

"You saw John Richards? How is he doing? Do they like their new home? What about . . ."

"No, I did not see John Richards. As I was going to say . . ."

Or what about the "cross-examiner"? He listens so well that when he responds to what you're saying you feel as though you were going through the third degree . . .

"Say, I just returned from our vacation and we had the greatest time. We stopped at this park and spent two days observing a deer herd."

"Well, what kind of deer were they? Mule or whitetail?"

"Well, I don't know."

"You don't know? Don't you know the difference? Didn't the guide explain the difference between the two? Well, in order to tell the difference you . . ."

Before long you probably wish that you had never seen any deer herd and you certainly wish you had never brought the subject up to your cross-examining friend.

These are just a few of the problems that you may encounter (or cause) because of non-listening.

Listen to what the Word of God has to say about listening:

He who answers a matter before he hears the facts, it is folly and shame to him (Prov. 18:13, *Amplified*).

A good verse for husbands and wives to commit to memory is James 1:19: every husband and wife should . . . *be quick to hear (a ready listener), slow to speak, slow to take offense and to get angry* (*Amplified*).

WHAT DO YOU THINK? #29

1. During the next few days try this experiment. Spend thirty minutes alone with your spouse and set aside everything else. First the wife has five minutes in which she will talk about anything she wants to. During that five minutes the husband must listen, he cannot talk and he must try to think of nothing except what his wife is saying to him. He should not try to daydream or think of what he would like to say in return. At the end of five minutes, switch roles. Now the husband talks and the wife listens. Switch back and forth every five minutes so that each spouse has at least three opportunities to talk and three opportunities to listen. At the end of thirty minutes, discuss your reactions and thoughts concerning this kind of activity. How can you apply this experience to your usual pattern of communicating?

Confucius Say, "Spouse with Horse Sense Never Becomes Nag"

When trying to communicate with your mate, keep in mind the ironic fact that too much talking can be as bad as too little. If you have adequately discussed a problem or a subject, drop it and move on. Do not restate your case and your conclusions over and over again. Too often you can create a bigger problem if you talk too much. Proverbs puts this nicely, if a bit bluntly: *Don't talk so much. You keep putting your foot in your mouth. Be sensible and turn off the flow!* (Prov. 10:19, *TLB*).

A typical form of "too much talking" is nagging—constantly harping or hassling your mate for one reason or another. A technical definition is "critical faulting"—but whatever you call it, nagging usually doesn't work. It irritates

and frustrates both marriage partners—the nagger as well as the "naggee."

You may have heard the quip, "The wife who uses good horse sense never turns out to be a nag." According to a national survey conducted by a leading magazine, the thing that irritates most men more than anything else is the wife's nagging.

On the other hand, men nag just as much as women. You may have said something like this yourself recently: "Nagging is the only way I know of to get my spouse to respond. And it's the same with the kids. If I don't tell them a dozen times and remind over and over again, the job never gets done!"

It's true that spouses and children especially seem to "need to be nagged." But perhaps there is a better way. If you do a lot of nagging, do you enjoy it? Is it really doing the job? If you're not happy with nagging, why continue to use an ineffective method? Consider the possibility that you may have conditioned your spouse and your children not to respond to you unless you nag—repeat and repeat and increase the volume as you do so.

If you have to say things a half-dozen times or more before you get any action your spouse is either: (1) not paying attention; (2) doesn't believe you mean anything the first time you speak.

How then can you gain your spouse's attention and not have to repeat and repeat? Perhaps your husband is sitting there watching the tube and you need to get a message through. Your problem is he's watching the Cowboys and the Redskins and that's an awful lot of opposition for any message—even yours. Use this simple strategy, however, and you'll score every time. Roll out to the left around his recliner, cut straight downfield and wind up standing right in front of the television set. If you really want to put on the pressure, *turn off* the television set. Your spouse's attention is guaranteed.

Or maybe your wife is engrossed in planning the big dinner party for Saturday night and you need to give her the word on servicing the car before you leave for work. The last thing she wants to hear is about what oil needs changing and where the grease has to go. So, go up to her and try looking her right in the eye as you talk to her. Perhaps you may want to put your hand on her shoulder (better yet, put your arms around her waist) and tell her what you have to say. There are all kinds of ways—some of them pleasant—to be something else than a nagger. Be creative and experiment. And keep Solomon's advice in mind: . . . *a nagging wife annoys like constant dripping* (Prov. 19:13, *TLB*). That much-married king also said: *It is better to dwell in a corner of the housetop [on the flat oriental roof, exposed to all kinds of weather] than in a house shared with a nagging, quarrelsome and faultfinding woman* (Prov. 21:9, *Amplified*).

WHAT DO YOU THINK? #30

1. List five things that you have asked (or nagged) your mate about that he or she has not changed or improved one bit. Why do you want your mate to change in these areas? Would the changes bring his or her behavior or attitude into closer harmony with Scripture? How else could you get your mate to change rather than to "keep mentioning it" (nagging)?

2. List five things that your mate has asked (or nagged) you about but you have not changed either because you could not or did not wish to do so.

3. Of the items listed for question 2, which ones could you have corrected if you had really wanted to do so?

4. Look at the items you have listed in your answer to question 3. Specify in detail your reasons for not making the changes suggested by your mate. Are your reasons valid? Have you honestly prayed about your decision to not make these changes? Would any of these changes bring your life closer to the teaching of Scripture?

5. For each of the items listed in your answer to question 1, put down the reasons why, in your opinion, your mate does not attempt to make the changes that you constantly suggest.

Don't Jump to Conclusions

Almost everyone knows the old joke about putting your brain in gear with your tongue before you start talking, but a lot of people seem to be unable to do this. They are quick to speak, and then spend a lot of time regretting what they said.

As the Scripture advises, *be . . . slow to speak* (See Jas. 1:19.) Think first. Don't be hasty in what you say. Control yourself and when you do talk, speak in such a way that your spouse can understand you and accept what you have to say.

Two more pieces of advice from Solomon fit in very well here:

He who guards his mouth and his tongue keeps himself from troubles (Prov. 21:23, *Amplified*).

Do you see a man who is hasty in his words? There is more hope of a [self-confident] fool than of him (Prov. 29:20, *Amplified*).

What these verses both say is that if you want to destroy a mate's self-esteem, just go off half-cocked and leap to conclusions before looking into things and finding out what's really happening. On the other hand, if you want to build your mate's self-esteem take James' advice (which, perhaps, should be part of every couple's marriage vows):

Be quick to hear (a ready listener), slow to speak, slow to take offense and to get angry (Jas. 1:19, *Amplified*).

Jumping to conclusions is a favorite sport in just about any setting, but it's particularly easy to do in a marriage.

She says, "Honey, I was out shopping today and I stopped in this cute little dress shop and I had the best time. . . ." He explodes: "What! You blew a bundle of money on some new clothes? You know we can't afford it!" (Actual situation: she tried on a few dresses and didn't buy a thing.)

Or he says: "Say, I was talking with some of the boys at the office and they're planning to get up this foursome Saturday and I. . . ."

And so she snaps: "You're going golfing when you've got all that trim to paint and the yard is beginning to look like an annex for Jungleland, U.S.A.?" (Actual situation: he turned the boys at the office down because he "had a lot of work to do at home.")

The illustrations go on and on and on. And self-esteem in both marriage partners suffers because of it.

Not only is it important to take your time when you feel yourself going into your "jump to conclusions" crouch . . . but on the positive side it helps to make the right kind of remarks at the right time. As Solomon put it, . . . *a word spo-*

NOT THIS...

BUT THIS...

ken at the right moment, how good it is! (Prov. 15:23, *Amplified*).

The illustrations (and opportunities) are endless as far as marriage is concerned. One obvious area where husbands can't say enough at the right moment is when complimenting their little woman's appearance. Instead of waiting for her to pry approval out of you about her hair, dress, cooking, etc., take a little more notice of your wife and pay her sincere compliments without having to have them solicited. A compliment coming from a husband, a spontaneous compliment, is worth a hundred times more in self-esteem value than the typical grunt: "Oh, yes . . . looks very nice. . . ."

As for the wives, they should never forget that their husbands are just as vain as they are (and more so). They also like compliments on their appearance and, again, it's better to do it at a spontaneous moment rather than wait till he is just putting on his new suit. All of us have the built-in resistance to compliments when they're given at those times, "when a compliment is expected." Learn to give compliments when they're not expected, and they'll be worth much more on the self-esteem market with your mate.

Disagree? Yes. Disrespect? No!

Always show respect for your mate's opinions even when you disagree. As already mentioned, no husband and wife can agree all of the time. But that doesn't mean they can't respect each other for their opinions and be willing to listen to one another. As Voltaire said, "I disapprove of what you say, but I will defend to the death your right to say it." You may not want to get that oratorical the next time you and your spouse disagree, but whatever you do, don't come up with such typical gems as:

"You're out to lunch."

"I just can't *believe* you!" (meaning "I don't question your veracity, just your right to belong to the human race").

"Oh, come on, don't get on that junk again."

A well-known TV comedian has gained fame and fortune with the line: "I don't get no respect." Perhaps one reason for his success is that so many husbands and wives identify completely with the idea of "not getting much respect." Paul must have had husbands and wives particularly in mind when he wrote: *Never act from motives of rivalry or personal vanity, but in humility think more of one another than you do of yourselves. None of you should think only of his own affairs, but each should learn to see things from other people's point of view* (Phil. 2:3,4, *Phillips*).

WHAT DO YOU THINK? #31

1. Think of several instances in which you showed respect for your spouse's ideas, opinions, or beliefs in the last week:

2. Think of several instances in which you may have shown disrespect for your spouse's opinions or ideas or beliefs in the last week:

3. Talk together with your mate about "respect for each other's opinions." If apologies are in order, make them. If gratitude or compliments are in order because both of you do respect one another, don't hold back on that, either! Remember— . . . *a word spoken at the right moment, how good it is!* (Prov. 15:23, *Amplified*).

Deal in Potential—Not the Past

Don't limit your mate by what he or she has done in the past that hasn't measured up or met completely with your approval. Are you guilty of putting your spouse in a pigeonhole? Check yourself and see if you ever (or often) make comments like these:

"He never understands me."

"She doesn't listen to what I say."

"He just won't change."

"She says one thing and then does another."

"I just can't reach him . . . he's hopeless."

If you've used any comments like these, ask yourself, "Would my spouse make the same statements about me? Do I do what I accuse my spouse of doing?"

The Christian couple will not stereotype or pigeonhole one another if they remember the key truth from the New Testament: God is far more interested in what a person can be than in what a person has been.

"Do you see other people in the process of becoming something better or do you see them as bound by their past —what they have (or haven't) done or said (especially to you)? . . . It is easy to stereotype others. You can place them in neat little pigeonholes like 'sloppy,' 'talk too much,' 'dishonest,' 'undependable,' 'unfair,' etc. . . . Christianity, however, deals in *potential,* and what a person can *become,* not only what he *is.* This is the heart of the gospel. If God had dealt with us strictly on the basis of our past, He would never have sent Christ to die for our sins. But God loved us. He saw us as persons of worth, value, with potential. He forgave, He keeps on forgiving, always looking forward to what we can become if we respond to the opportunity we have in Christ." (4)

Don't Force Your Spouse to Be Your Carbon Copy

If you truly love your mate, you will not demand (subtly

DON'T LABEL YOUR MATE

or otherwise) that he or she become a modified version of your ideas or a revised edition of yourself. Set your mate free to be an individual with his or her own opinions. Always guard against giving your mate the impression that you love him or her more when he or she agrees with you. Keep in mind that ". . . all of us are self-conscious. Our image of self is directly related to how we feel, what we do, things we like. Criticize a person's viewpoint, taste, ideas and you criticize *him,* no matter how much you may mean otherwise.

"Before turning your guns (especially your spiritual guns) on someone's ideas, attitudes, actions, ask yourself a couple of questions: am I trying to help this person or am I really trying to impose my value system on him? Do I respect and like this person for what he is, or am I trying to make him over to suit my idea of what is respectable, likable or spiritual?" (5)

Pray for One Another

Pray for each other privately and, if you can, pray together for each other. There is a lot of talk in Christian circles about husbands and wives "reading the Bible and praying together" but it is questionable how many really do so. To paraphrase the well-known slogan, "If a husband and wife will pray together they will not only stay together but they will communicate much more effectively."

In the Old Testament, the Israelites demanded and finally got a king—Saul—to lead them against the many enemies that surrounded them. Samuel, the last of the judges, reluctantly agreed to find and crown Saul; but again and again he warned the Israelites that they should be sure to follow God and not depend entirely on their new king. In 1 Samuel 12, Samuel makes an impassioned speech to remind the Israelite people of their responsibilities to God and not to get carried away with a recent victory over enemies led by King Saul. The people respond by asking—practically begging—Samuel to continue to pray for them and intercede for them to God.

Samuel responds by saying, . . . *Far be it from me that I should sin against the Lord by ending my prayers for you* (1 Sam. 12:23, *TLB*).

Husband and wife should spend some time studying this Old Testament passage together. Samuel had spiritual responsibilities for his people, which were given to him by God. When husband and wife take their marriage vows, they are given spiritual responsibility to one another, as well as physical, mental and emotional responsibilities. With all of the challenges and pressures on marriage today, husband and wife should both guard against "sinning against the Lord" (not to mention each other) by failing to pray for one another. As Paul Tournier points out: "It is only when a husband and wife pray together before God that they find the secret of true harmony, that the difference in their temperaments, their ideas, and their tastes enriches their home instead of endangering it. There will be no further question of one imposing his will on the other, or of the other giving in for the sake of peace. Instead, they will together seek God's will, which alone will ensure that each will be fully able to develop his personality. . . . When each of the marriage partners seeks quietly before God to see his own faults, recognizes his sin, and asks the forgiveness of the other, marital problems are no more. Each learns to speak the other's language, and to meet him halfway, so to speak. Each holds back those harsh little words which one is apt to utter when one is right, but which are said in order to injure. Most of all, a couple rediscovers complete mutual confidence, because, in meditating in prayer together they learn to become absolutely honest with each other. . . . This is the price to be paid if partners very different from each other are to combine their gifts instead of setting them against each other." (6)

All of the ideas and suggestions in this book will be of little use to the Christian couple if they neglect prayer, one for another. In fact, many of the ideas and suggestions in this book, especially those that suggest or imply changes that either spouse must make, will be impossible to achieve or use without prayer. God is the One who changes a marriage—not manuals or books!

There is one other guideline to help you and your mate apply this book to your marriage. Better communication depends upon change—changes in both of you. Changing some of your patterns may take a long time, but change is possible through Jesus Christ. To say that you are so set in your ways that you cannot change is to contradict the good news that Jesus Christ can and will make us new creatures.

We all change in proportion to the effort we put forth to try to change. As we let the Word of God sink into our hearts and minds we will change. We will remember what to do because the Scripture is a part of our lives and through Scripture we have a built-in guide for change. How can we learn to communicate, to build self-esteem in each other, to love and understand one another? By reading God's Word and following His rules. We must try our best to find God and we must not wander off from His instructions. We must think much about God's words and store them in our hearts. God's Word will hold us back from sinning against one another by failing to communicate. (See Ps. 119:9,11.)

And as Dwight Small puts it, we should not overidealize the magic power of communication. Small cautions: ". . . that no amount of communication can make marriage perfect, and therefore we should not expect it. God is perfect, the ideal of Christian marriage is perfect, and the means God puts at the disposal of Christian couples are perfect. Yet there is no perfect marriage, no perfect communication in marriage. The glory in Christian marriage is in accepting the life-long task of making a continual adjustment within the disorder of human existence, ever working to improve communication skills necessary to this task, and seeking God's enabling power in it all." (7)

Keep in mind also that communication is a means, not an end. The end of marriage is not communication. The end of marriage is love—love for God and love for one another. Notice the order here. "When married people think only of happiness, they fall short of communicating the highest love of all. They, in fact, idolize each other, taking gratification in possessing and adoring their idol. Such devotion leads them away from God and from the Christian experience of love, since the two are dearer than God is to them. The highest form of love liberates two people from idolatry, keeping them from dominating and possessing each other and from demanding utter devotion as the price of love. Only God is worthy of utter devotion. So a couple are not to live entirely for each other, but must recognize that all love has its source in God. As loving husbands and wives, married partners are servants who mediate God's love, letting their love for each other serve a higher end." (8)

Today everyone realizes that you can have a marriage without love. Some are advocating love without marriage. Neither option is very attractive to the Christian. Love doesn't come automatically in marriage, but love matures in marriage as two people work to communicate.

WHAT'S YOUR PLAN?

1. Sit down with your marriage partner and talk over the principles discussed in this chapter. Make a mutual commitment to try to follow them in the future. Agree to be accountable to one another and devise a plan for regular evaluation of how well you are succeeding.

2. If either one of you violates any of the principles, how will you handle it? List ideas for a procedure that both of you will be able to accept and carry out.

3. Study the "Marriage Communication Guidelines" on the next page. Go through each of the ten guidelines and all of the suggested Scripture verses. Talk about each one. Add other guidelines that you can remember from reading this book, which are not in the list. Then sign your names to the guidelines and put in the date. For the best effect, both marriage partners should sign the same page in a copy of this book. You may want to cut the page from the book and put it up on your bulletin board or other conspicuous spot in the house.

Marriage Communication Guidelines

Proverbs 18:21; 25:11; Job 19:2; James 3:8-10; 1 Peter 3:10

1. Be a ready listener and do not answer until the other person has finished talking. Proverbs 18:13; James 1:19

2. Be slow to speak. Think first. Don't be hasty in your words. Speak in such a way that the other person can understand and accept what you say.
Proverbs 15:23,28; 21:23; 29:20; James 1:19

3. Speak the truth always but do it in love. Do not exaggerate. Ephesians 4:15,25; Colossians 3:9

4. Do not use silence to frustrate the other person. Explain why you are hesitant to talk at this time.

5. Do not become involved in quarrels. It is possible to disagree without quarreling.
Proverbs 17:14; 20:3; Romans 13:13; Ephesians 4:31

6. Do not respond in anger. Use a soft and kind response.
Proverbs 14:29; 15:1; 25:15; 29:11; Ephesians 4:26,31

7. When you are in the wrong, admit it and ask for forgiveness. James 5:16. When someone confesses to you, tell them you forgive them. Be sure it is *forgotten* and not brought up to the person.
Proverbs 17:9; Ephesians 4:32; Colossians 3:13; 1 Peter 4:8

8. Avoid nagging. Proverbs 10:19; 17:9; 20:5

9. Do not blame or criticize the other person. Instead, restore . . . encourage . . . edify. Romans 14:13; Galatians 6:1; 1 Thessalonians 5:11. If someone verbally attacks, criticizes or blames you, do not respond in the same manner.
Romans 12:17,21; 1 Peter 2:23; 3:9

10. Try to understand the other person's opinion. Make allowances for differences. Be concerned about their interests. Philippians 2:1-4; Ephesians 4:2

Our Agreement to Follow These Guidelines

Name ______________________________ *Date*________________

Name ______________________________ *Date*________________

bibliography and resources

INTRODUCTION

1. Richard Lessor, *Love, Marriage and Trading Stamps*. (Argus Publications, 1971), p. 7

2. Charles Shedd, *Letters to Phillip*. (Spire Books, 1969), pp. 82,83.

CHAPTER 1

1. J. A. Fritze, *The Essence of Marriage*. (Zondervan, 1969), adapted from p. 24.

2. David Augsburger, *Cherishable: Love and Marriage*. (Herald Press, 1971), p. 16.

3. Dwight Small, *After You've Said I Do*. (Fleming H. Revell, 1968), pp. 11,16.

4. Dwight Small, *After You've Said I Do*. (Fleming H. Revell, 1968), p. 51.

5. Dwight Small, *Design for Christian Marriage*. (Fleming H. Revell, 1959), p. 26.

CHAPTER 2

1. "What Did St. Paul Want?" Dwight Small. From *His* magazine, May 1973, p. 18.

2. "What Did St. Paul Want?", Gladys Hunt. From *His* magazine, May 1973, p. 14.

CHAPTER 3

1. Nathan W. Ackerman, M.D., *The Psychodynamics of Family Life*. (Basic Books, 1958), pp. 110-115.

2. James Jauncey, *Magic in Marriage*. (Zondervan, 1966), pp. 110,111.

3. Lionel A. Whiston, *Are You Fun to Live With?* (Word Books, 1968), pp. 126,127.

4. William L. Coleman, "Spousehold Hints . . . His . . . Hers" from *Moody Monthly*, February, 1973, p. 47.

5. David Augsburger, *Be All You Can Be*. (Creation House Publishers, 1970), pp. 74,75.

CHAPTER 4

1. Reuel Howe, *Herein Is Love*. (Judson Press, 1961), see p. 100.

2. Adapted from *After You've Said I Do*. Dwight H. Small. (Fleming H. Revell, 1968), See pp. 106,107,112.

3. Adapted from *The Art of Understanding Yourself*, Cecil Osborne. (Zondervan, 1967.) See chapter 9.

CHAPTER 5

1. John Powell, *Why Am I Afraid to Tell You Who I Am?* (Argus Communications). Adapted from pp. 54-62.

2. Dwight Small, *After You've Said I Do*. (Fleming H. Revell, 1968), p. 244.

CHAPTER 6

1. William C. Menninger, *Behind Many Flaws of Society*. (*National Observer*, August 31, 1964), p. 18.

2. Spiros Zodhiates, *Pursuit of Happiness*. (Eerdmans, 1966), p. 270.

3. David Augsburger, *Be All You Can Be*. (Creation House), p. 60.

4. John Powell, *Why Am I Afraid to Tell You Who I Am?* (Argus Communications, 1969), p. 155.

5. William C. Menninger, *Ibid.*, p. 18.
6. David Augsburger, *Ibid.*, pp. 31,32.

CHAPTER 7

1. James A. Hadfield, *Psychology and Morals.* (Barnes and Noble, Inc., 1964), p. 35.
2. Adapted from *Why Am I Afraid to Tell You Who I Am?* John Powell. (Argus Communications, 1969), pp. 91,92.
3. Robert McFarland and John Burton, *Learning for Loving.* (Zondervan, 1969), p. 93.
4. Dwight Small, *After You've Said I Do.* (Fleming H. Revell, 1968), p. 75.
5. Virginia Satir, *Conjoint Family Therapy.* (Science and Behavior Books, Inc., 1967), p. 73.
6. Howard J. Clinebell, *The Intimate Marriage.* (Harper & Row, 1970), p. 99.
7. Dwight Small, *After You've Said I Do.* (Fleming H. Revell), pp. 137,154.

CHAPTER 8

1. John Edmund Haggai, *How to Win over Worry.* (Zondervan, 1959), p. 17.
2. Lionel Whiston, *Are You Fun to Live With?* (Word Books, 1968), pp. 141,142.
3. Bruce Larson, *Living on the Growing Edge.* (Zondervan, 1968), p. 56.
4. Dwight Small, *After You've Said I Do.* (Fleming H. Revell, 1966), p. 79.

CHAPTER 9

1. Adapted from Albert Ellis and Robert Harper, *Creative Marriage.* (Lyle Stuart, 1961), pp. 190-191.
2. Howard Clinebell, *The Intimate Marriage.* (Harper & Row, 1970), p. 93.
3. John Edmund Haggai, *How to Win over Worry.* (Zondervan, 1959), pp. 63,64.

CHAPTER 10

1. Dorothy Briggs, *Your Child's Self-Esteem: the Key to His Life*. (Doubleday and Co.), p. 3.

2. John Drakeford, *Games Husbands and Wives Play*. (Word Publishers, 1970), p. 73.

3. Paul Tournier, *To Understand Each Other*. (John Knox Press, 1962), p. 58.

4. Fritz Ridenour, *How to Be a Christian Without Being Religious*. (Regal Books, 1967), pp. 147,148.

5. Fritz Ridenour, *Ibid.*, p. 126.

6. Paul Tournier, *The Healing of Persons*. (Harper & Row Publishers, 1965), pp. 88,89.

7. Dwight Small, *After You've Said I Do*. (Revell, 1968), p. 81.

8. Dwight Small, *Ibid.*, p. 235.

The publishers do not necessarily endorse the entire contents of all publications referred to in this book.